THE
RACE

*I have fought the good fight,
I have finished the race, I have kept
the faith. Henceforth there is laid up for
me the crown of righteousness,
which the Lord, the righteous judge,
will award to me on that Day,
and not only to me but also to all who
have loved his appearing.*

———————————

2 Timothy 4:7-8

John White

THE RACE

The Christian way
in faith and practice

Inter-Varsity Press

INTER-VARSITY PRESS

38 De Montfort Street, Leicester LE1 7GP

First British edition 1984

Jointly published in Australia with Lancer Books, P.O. Box 115, Flemington Markets, N.S.W. 2129, Australia.

British Library Cataloguing in Publication Data
White, John, *1924 Mar. 5 –*
    The Race: the Christian way in faith and practice
    1. Christian life
    I. Title
    248.4   BV4501.2
    UK ISBN 0-85110-462-2
    Australian ISBN 85892-248-7

Printed and bound in Great Britain by
Cox & Wyman Ltd, Reading

Inter-Varsity Press is the publishing division of the Universities and Colleges Christian Fellowship (formerly the Inter-Varsity Fellowship), a student movement linking Christian Unions in universities and colleges throughout the United Kingdom and the Republic of Ireland, and a member movement of the International Fellowship of Evangelical Students. For information about local and national activities write to UCCF, 38 De Montfort Street, Leicester LE1 7GP.

To my children (in-laws and out-laws!)

Acknowledgments

Earlier versions of many of the chapters in this book appeared in the following periodicals:

Brown Gold Publications—"Parable of the Orange Trees," used by permission.

Decision magazine—"Private Devotions: Why?" (January 1980). ©1979 John White.

Eternity—"Witnessing Is *Not* Brainwashing" (February 1965). Reprinted by permission of *Eternity* magazine, ©1965, Evangelical Ministries, Inc., 1716 Spruce Street, Philadelphia, PA 19103.

HIS magazine—"Walk into Light" (April 1962); "Dilemma" (November 1962); "Embarrassing Doctrine?" (February 1963); *"Dos Comunistas"* (October 1964); "Priscilla and Apollos" (February 1965); "The Four Travelers" (March 1965); "Missions and Proselytism" (November 1967); "Parrot Fish" (June 1969); "The God of White-Hot Rage" (November 1979); "Tickle-and-Tease: The Lure of Pornography" (May 1981).

Inter-Varsity magazine (UK)—"Metamorphosis" (Autumn 1963).

Moody Monthly—"The Power of Forgiveness" (November 1962); "God's Perfect Peace" (December 1962); "The Christian and Gossip" (November 1963); "Absolute Lord" (October 1964); "Self—The Unjolly Giant" (September 1968).

The Sunday School Times—"Can Unity Exist at the Expense of Truth?" (11 August 1962); "Born of a Virgin" (8 December 1962); "What Evangelicals Believe about the Bible" (12 January 1963); "Christ's Death" (30 March 1963); "What to Do When You Have 'The Blues' " (29 February 1964); "Faith Is" (18 December 1965); "I Dare You to Examine It!" (25 December 1965); "Is God a 'Human Invention?" (1 January 1966); "Fountain of Fatherhood" (8 January 1966); "Sin Now, Pay Later" (15 January 1966); "God Is Spirit" (22 January 1966); "You and Your Guilt Feelings" (5 February 1966).

Preface

_____I was startled when I met them. Startled by the number of them. You sire children one at a time and grow confused after a while about matters like numbers, ages, characters, faces.

I didn't recognize them all immediately. After all, I had not seen some of them for years and was a little embarrassed by the undeniable evidence of my promiscuity. Was I really responsible for such a crowd?

I confess that when Andy Le Peau had suggested that he hunt them up I was not very enthusiastic. I had not realized there were enough to be worth hunting. But like bunches of pale prisoners they emerged from dusty magazine archives to confront me and plead their cause with totally unexpected articulateness and vigor. "We still exist," they said resentfully, "and we see no reason why we should have to go on living in obscurity."

I was also embarrassed when they auditioned for us (you know the mixed feelings parents have when their kids perform in public) but at the same time more impressed than I cared to let them see. I even felt a glimmer of pride. "Yes, you need a little sprucing up," I thought to myself, "but maybe there's potential in your working together."

"You were passionate when we were conceived," they pleaded. "Why so cold now? Don't you realize we've inherited your passion? We want to do a road show, and you've no right to stop us. It's not that we're jealous of the one or two of us that have made a bit of a name for themselves. But we've got something to offer, and some of us only gave one performance. United we sta—..."

"Yes, but just how united are you?" I demanded.

"We're family!"

"Unfortunately, I can't deny that. But whether you're united or not is another question altogether. Families rarely are."

"Well, *we* are!" Defiance flared from their eyes. "We work together as a team. In Act I we lay the foundations of the whole plot. It's a solid foundation."

"So?"

"Well, the other three acts follow in logical sequence. Given the dramatic truth of Act I, the rest *has* to follow; but there's a tension—"

"Yes, that's my point, tension—"

"We're talking about *dramatic* tension. You see, you only have a soap opera if you don't begin with truth. But truth has to produce action. And sometimes it doesn't. So that's where the tension arises. Will it work out? How can it be worked out? In this case it really does."

"You're not convincing me. Some of you fight. Others of you just echo one another's sentiments."

"That's not true!" they yelled. "Anyway, if Andy—"

"If Andy what?"

"We're talking about a four-act musical, right? With Andy as director/producer. We're calling it *The Race*."

"The Race?"

"Yes. People need help with running it. They know they

should. If that isn't clear in Act I, it becomes obvious in Act II. But the question is how? In Acts III and IV . . ."

"Yes, but—a musical? I don't think Andy's interested in mere entertainment—"

"*It's Andy's idea!* Anyway it's not just entertainment. There will be light touches, here and there. You can't have tension all the way through. But we've also got a message. A coherent message. It's worth giving and we give it well. At least we could do with a half-decent director. Take Act I again—"

"Let me see the script."

Act I impressed me. There were holes here and there, but it was better than I could have hoped. It stirred ideas in me that had lain dormant. There was a solidity, a compactness, a doctrinal backbone to it.

"It may be Andy's idea, but you're *my* kids. And I'm not going to let you make a fool of me. I don't care what Andy says. He can turn you down if he wants to, but he can't put your show on without *my* permission."

I felt hostility in their silence, but I went on perusing the script.

"Some of this stuff—"

"Yes?"

"Well, in Act III, for instance, one or two of the lyrics sound like stuff from *The Fight*."

"Similar, but different. New content. Fresh."

"You'd still be making me sort of repeat myself here and there."

"We resent that! Talk about vanity! We may be your children, but we're *unique*. We're your kids not your clones. We have our own thing to do."

There was silence on my part this time. "O.K.," I muttered after a while, "but you're still not the bosses. If this show is to get on the road, *you do what we say!*"

Yet inside of me I knew they were right. I wish I could be

there on the opening night because I suspect they'll make it. My prayers are with them, anyway. I began to realize that perhaps their life came from God, not just from me. If so, some people who see the show will go away and start running. The Race. The Long Race. To its conclusion.

Part I
Christian
Beliefs

1
God: Beyond
and Very Near

_____You may not know it, but you carry it with you everywhere you go. You will never lose it, for it is part of you. It is always turned on and the switch is inaccessible. It was born when you were born. It will go on working even after your body dies.

In what we call our space-time continuum the only thing you could do would be to try to ignore it. Noises around you might help drown it out. Some people try to escape it by plunging into hectic activity, but it can pierce the most raucous background, outstrip the fastest runner. Yet some people are successful in learning not to hear it. Sometimes for years.

Paradoxically it can grow hardest to detect when you most long to hear it. That may be your fault. You may need to relearn how to listen. It will be there, still functioning. It is God's communication unit. Unbreakable. Inescapable. Not subject to our whims or moods.

And when the most convincing arguments against God's existence have been stated, he ignores the arguments and goes on speaking through it. Christians have always known about God's communication units. But more important is the existence of the God who speaks through them. Who is he, after all? What is he like?

The Bible begins with God. And so does a great deal of human thinking. His existence is the central question of life. Some say, however, that we created God in our own image. They mean not only that God is a human invention but also that the invention is not entirely original (as human inventions never are). God is merely humanity blown bigger. Let's trace the thinking that leads to this conclusion so that we can evaluate it fairly.

If we try to create something entirely new and different *in essence*, different from everything that is, we fail. We must use materials that already exist and ideas we have borrowed from our observations. What we produce is a modification of other things. It's not *new* at all. In fact, we can't even *think* of something "new" in this sense. Whenever we try, we find ourselves thinking either of clouds of gas or space—or of alterations of things we've already experienced. We can only conceive ideas based on our actual experience. So if we did invent the idea of God, God would be the kind of idea people could readily grasp. One concept would lead to another, much in the same way as in math. Even calculus presents no problems if we've grasped the ideas leading up to it.

It would be possible, in fact, to conceive of a line of beings leading, without a break, from man to "God." Those at our end of the line would be pretty much like us. And even the "God" at the other end would have distinctly recognizable properties. At least we could see how he was derived from our experience and could be described in human terms as bigger, or *much, much* more powerful, or less personal, and the like.

The question, then, that we must answer is: Could we have invented the God of the Bible? We can certainly see how some concepts of God could be human inventions. But is it also true of the God of the Scriptures?

The Bible is plain. With one voice Bible writers declare the infinite qualitative difference between God and us. When Moses asked God what his name was (another way of asking what he was really like, God answered, "I AM WHO I AM" (Ex 3:14). This could be translated, "There is nothing you could compare me with."

Holy, Holy, Holy

The word *holiness* denotes God's differentness, his otherness. We often think of holiness as a sort of infinitely superior goodness. It is much more. Two elements are of special importance. We've already mentioned the one—his inconceivableness. Theologians call it his *transcendence*. While God has made himself both real and close to those who believe in Christ (what theologians call *immanence*), we would never dare claim to understand God. A baby may know and enjoy the nearness of his mother, but he does not thereby comprehend her. And the gap preventing us from understanding God is far wider. Dizzy with its infinite span, Paul cries out, "How unsearchable are his judgments and how inscrutable his ways!" (Rom 11:33).

The other aspect of God's holiness we would not have invented either—his moral perfection. By this we are not just implying that we give him top grades for keeping all the rules. We mean that he is free from all moral limitations. God is not holy because he obeys certain laws which define the difference between right and wrong. Those rules are himself! He gave birth to the very quality that we call righteousness before time was. Purity, faithfulness, mercy and lovingkindness are his inventions. The rules merely describe, dimly and imperfectly, what God is.

As you see, we could quickly tie ourselves into intellectual knots discussing God's holiness. We might get into a complex argument with an atheist friend. But one who catches the least glimmer of what holiness means can't be bothered with arguing about it any more than a man in love wants to argue about the existence of women. A very different experience engages all his attention.

Kenneth Grahame catches something of this experience in his classic story for children, *The Wind in the Willows*. Mole and Rat after a night of anguish encounter Friend and Helper at dawn on an island on the River Thames. We are told that as Mole looked,

> . . . he lived. And still as he lived, he wondered. "Rat!" he found breath to whisper, shaking. "Are you afraid?"
>
> "Afraid?" murmured the Rat, his eyes shining with unutterable love—"Afraid! Of *Him?* Oh, never, never! And yet—and yet—Oh, Mole, I am *afraid!*"

Holiness, you see, is easier *felt* than *telt*.

Perhaps that is why the Bible speaks most often about God's holiness in poetry, song and prayer—the languages of worship. It may be a reason, too, why we should approach the study of such passages not only with our minds alert but with our hearts bowed and still. For the infinite God is waiting to show some of his holiness to us.

God Is Spirit

Holiness is not the only word the Bible uses to describe God. It also says he is *Spirit*. This is a strange expression for modern men and women. For us the word *nonmaterial* is almost the same as *nonexistent*. The only kind of reality we know is formed of mass and energy. The absence of these means nothingness. Nonexistence.

Abstract ideas, you might argue, are nonmaterial reality. You can't touch ideas any more than you can weigh them. Yet they're *there*, so to speak. They're real. They are also independent of our conceiving them.

But in a sense ideas, too, are material. You can't have a

thought without a material thinker. There's no such thing as an idea without a movement of electrons along cerebral pathways. For this reason materialists claim that, although ideas may themselves be nonmaterial, they arise from matter. Matter is basic to ideas.

Yet the God of the Bible is declared to be the nonmaterial *source* of matter. He existed before there were human brains to think thoughts about him. In fact, he created human brains. In the same way as people invent computers and not merely the coded information stored electronically inside the computer, so God is much more than an idea in human brains. The whole human race could perish and its ideas be snuffed out like candles. But God would exist.

Instead of using words like *nonmaterial* (a negative term, yet one we understand), the Bible speaks of God as *Spirit* (a positive term we do not fully understand). We can't think of what spirit is any more than we can see the wind. Many of us form vague pictures in our minds of something that floats and fills space. Probably we will one day laugh at our concepts. Yet in the meantime it is comforting to know that we are not called to understand spirit but to *know* God the Spirit.

Two facts about the Spirit are key. The first is that the Spirit of God is more than an abstraction. He is a Person. He teaches (Jn 14:26). He can feel grief (Eph 4:30). He rebukes us and reveals things to us (Jn 16:8-11).

The second fact is that the Spirit is alive. Ideas, of course, are said to live when they cause changes in society. They are dead when they are forgotten. But God is not an idea, and he is alive in a much more important sense.

Biological life (the only kind we are acquainted with) is self-reproducing. Flowers give seed from which more flowers grow. Bacteria, viruses, humans and frogs all reproduce after their kind. It is apparent from Scripture that biological life provides us with an analogy for conceiving spiritual life. Even its capacity to reproduce itself is an echo of the more powerful and significant form of life, the spiritual. God the Spirit begets sons (Jn 3:1-8). He begets them among human bipeds by planting the living seed of his Word in their hearts.

The vital energy of the life he imparts is so great that our character is changed. Men and women who have experienced spiritual rebirth are aware of a new force within them. Their friends become aware of it too—by change of behavior and even of faces. Such men and women are the sons and daughters of God in a quite literal sense. He has reproduced himself in them. Again, our minds reel to comprehend such thoughts, and our hearts leap that God loves us so.

Higher Personality

While God is unlike us, there are ways in which he is also like us. We have already noted that he is a Person. And we are persons. In this regard, however, modern thinkers, afraid of falling into the old trap of conceiving of a god who is too human, sometimes fall into the worse error of making him less than human. God may excel his creatures in sincerity and truth, they say, but, where personality is concerned, he is distinctly subhuman.

Such thinking is curiously at variance with our way of looking at, say, the animal kingdom. We are accustomed to speak of "higher" vertebrates and "lower" vertebrates, implying not only chronological and developmental scales, but (though we are quick to deny it) a scale of values. Higher animals are those which not only employ higher intelligence but also possess some of the attributes of personality.

Among the things that make up personality, for example, are emotions. Humans are superior to animals because of the range, intensity and infinite subtlety of their emotions, as well as their skills in both communicating and concealing them. Worms (so far as we can tell) have no fine shades of feeling. Dogs are way ahead of worms emotionally, yet we suspect that a dog's emotions are crude beside ours. Certainly his methods of communicating them— barking, jumping up and down, and whimpering—are direct and to the point. And he seems relatively incapable of concealing his feelings. Humans, on the other hand, feel grief more keenly and for longer periods. Too, we may express our grief by writing poetry—or we may hide it altogether.

Although the Bible makes clear that God is so superior to us that we shall never fully comprehend him, the picture it gives shows him to be not less but more personal than we are.

He is a Person. He is not a mighty, impersonal Thing but a *super*personal Being.

Therefore, if, as the Bible says, God did create us and create us in his image, then it stands to reason that God's personality is more vivid than ours—just as we are more real than our picture. And, since there are points of genuine comparison between God and us—as well as points of difference—it also stands to reason that the Holy Spirit should use such points to teach us what God is like.

Superb teacher that he is, the Spirit knows we grasp most readily ideas based on our own experience. He teaches us, for example, that God is both Father and fatherly. Once again we must beware of the pseudointellectual trap of saying that God isn't *really* a father, but that this concept helps make him more real to us if we learn to think of him in that way. On the contrary, he is the original Father—the fountain of fatherhood (Eph 3:14-15)! All the fine and meaningful things about human fathers are but feeble copies. A human father may melt inwardly as he watches his young children at play. But this is nothing compared to God's overflowing tenderness as he looks down on his children and nothing to the anguish he knows when we forsake him.

The concept of God as Father leaps to life in the book of Hosea. Few things fill a human father so full of emotion as helping his first baby to walk. "It was I who taught Ephraim to walk," God says, lamenting that the child has now forsaken him (Hos 11:3).

So deep and fierce are God's fatherly yearnings that he longs to acquire more sons and to bring back to him those who have wandered away. Like the father of the prodigal son, he waits on the road, searching the horizon for the return of the one who was lost, ready to welcome him home. If there is but the glimmer of desire and willingness on our part to come to him in humility and repentance, the God who is holy beyond our comprehension, the God who is Spirit yet the highest reality, the God whose wrath and compassion far surpass ours—this loving Father will not delay in revealing himself to us.

2
The God of White-Hot Rage

_____"The God of White-Hot Rage." Does my title sound extreme? Perhaps.

But you see, I'm not interested in the kind of God we *want* to believe in, but in the God who really is.

We Christians are idolators. In the last chapter I noted that our critics accuse us of making God in our own image —and to an extent they are right. We may not carve him out of wood, but we do try to forget the unpleasant parts of him and shape him to our personal comfort.

I once read an article by a man who called himself an evangelical yet talked about "the kind of God I would feel comfortable with." He, at least, was being honest about doing what we all do—making God into a sort of holy Teddy Bear.

I used to be distressed by the God of the Old Testament until I began to draw near to him. It has been a long, awesome process. God has never troubled to defend himself before my frightened inquiries. Instead he has chosen graciously to reveal himself so that, weeping and trembling, yet unspeakably uplifted and reassured, I have worshiped and adored him and cried, "Let God be God forever!"

If we have trouble coming to terms with the idea of an angry God, there may be at least three kinds of reasons. We may be troubled for psychological reasons, biblical reasons or theological reasons. Let's look at them one at a time.

The Psychological Problem

We may be bothered by the idea of an angry God because we know what our own anger is like. The matter may be complicated because we were taught that anger is innately evil. Certainly our human anger can be a vicious, evil, ugly thing. It's inconceivable to think of God as having that same guilt-provoking rage.

But there we go again creating God in our own image. We read into God's anger what we experience of our own. Yet God's anger is altogether unlike ours. His anger is against evil. All evil. Everywhere. Always. My anger is often about trivia.

I get mad when I'm frustrated. My pencil snaps for the fourth time in a row, or the man in front of me stalls at a stoplight while the cars behind me honk impatiently. God's pencils do not break. Honking cars do not perturb him. He is never frustrated, never in a hurry.

At other times I get angry because I'm uncertain about my position or feel insecure. When people disagree with my argument I begin to shout, because I have a deep, nasty fear that they may be right after all.

God is not insecure. He never gets upset.

Or I may get angry because I can't control people. Wives get angry when they can't control their husbands' embarrassing behavior in public. Husbands rage because they can't always stop their wives from "running the show."

Only God has the right to control people. And often he chooses not to because he has made men and women in his own image and given them the responsibility of choice. But

God is almighty. The problem of control, selfish or otherwise, doesn't exist for God.

Much of our anger arises from two basic sources: our sinful attitudes and our impotence. Since God is neither impotent nor sinful, such angers can never be attributed to him. He is omnipotent. He is holy.

There are times when we have every right to be angry. But when in our anger we behave with cruelty and a vicious lack of control, we are appalled by the sometimes irreparable damage we have done. We stare in dismay at the wreck of a lifelong friendship or weep over the final alienation of a child or parent. It was not that the anger was wrong, but that we could not control it and recklessly let it energize destructive sin.

God never loses his temper. Where the Bible talks about God's anger "waxing hot," it is using a literary device. God does not have a physical ear to hear, nor a physical arm to make bare. And his anger neither waxes nor wanes. "Waxing hot" makes it simpler for us to understand. But his anger, like everything else about God, is immutable, timeless, eternal.

Therefore we must not fall into the trap of supposing that the ugly things that torment us also torment God. God's anger is different from ours.

Yet God is still an angry God.

The Biblical Problem

We have gotten used to the New Testament. Many of us can negotiate our way skillfully through its passages about God's anger. It is only when we courageously read through the Old Testament that we are startled by things we hadn't faced in the New.

In the back of our minds the words *progressive revelation* may trouble us. What do they mean? Is there some truth to the idea that, as people's understanding of God matured and grew, they left behind the crude ideas of primitive Israel—the concept of a God who lost his temper? Now that Christ has come, gentle, loving, meek and mild, are we to understand that the New corrects the Old?

Progressive revelation can mean anything. To me it means that the bold outlines of God sketched in Genesis are progressively fleshed out in the rest of the Old Testament. The finer and glorious details are clarified in the New. But progression and change are not the same thing. God is not different from who he used to be.

How does God's rage in the Old Testament compare with his rage in the New? Some of my less conservative friends say, "Isaiah! Ah, *there* is a man who begins to understand the breadth of God! Mercy to all people, universal kindness! In Isaiah the gospel begins!" Does it? What my friends are doing is what I just accused us all of doing in the New Testament. They read selectively, delicately ignoring Isaiah's occasional lapses into "primitive" views of God.

But these references are plentiful. Isaiah 30:30 and 33 says: "And the LORD will cause his majestic voice to be heard and the descending blow of his arm to be seen, in furious anger and a flame of devouring fire, with a cloudburst and tempest and hailstones. . . . For a burning place has long been prepared; yea, for the king it is made ready, its pyre made deep and wide, with fire and wood in abundance; the breadth of the LORD, like a stream of brimstone, kindles it."

The verses are not isolated texts. They occur throughout the prophecy—indeed, throughout all the prophets. White-hot rage? My expression does not exaggerate what Scripture repeatedly says.

"But what of the New Testament?" you may ask. "Was not the Lord Jesus Christ the incarnate revelation of God's true nature? What of *his* life? What of *his* teaching?"

His teaching? How about the parable of the rich man and

Lazarus? "And in Hades, being in torment, he [the rich man] lifted up his eyes, and . . . called out . . . have mercy upon me . . . for I am in anguish in this flame" (Lk 16:23-24).

What about the gentle way he discussed theology with unbelieving Jews in the Temple? "You are of your father the devil, and your will is to do your father's desires. He was a murderer from the beginning" (Jn 8:44). Did he say it with a smile? Or tentatively?

Or how about his attitude at the purification of the Temple? The accounts can be compared in all four Gospels. Was he or was he not displaying wrath? Consider the details:

1. He was careful to prepare for physical violence. He made a whip of cords (Jn 2:15). If he wove with the same thoroughness with which he did everything else, it was a carefully made whip. We can be sure, then, that we are not dealing with an impulsive outburst of temper. The deed was planned. Yet can we deny that it was an angry deed?

2. It was a violent and forceful action. He drove everyone out of the Temple and overturned tables piled high with money (Jn 2:15).

3. His violence was exhibited against people as well as animals. Take the word *them* in John 2:15. To whom does it apply? To people, or to animals? Read verses 14 and 15 carefully. Whom did he find doing wrong? If verse 15 says that "he drove them all [out]" and the word *them* refers to the birds and animals, why does the whole phrase read "he drove them all [out], *with the sheep and oxen*"? Obviously, he drove out the *people* too.

You may say, "It doesn't actually say that he *lashed* the people." So what? If a man walks toward you with a whip in his hand, seizes your table and tips it up on end, and seizes the stool you are sitting on to throw you off (Mk 11:15)—does it really matter whether the whip lashes you or not? What is inescapable is that physical violence is directed against you.

Or do you suppose that Jesus said, "You know, I hate to have to do this to you fellows, but if you will excuse me . . ."? What expression was on his face as he said, "My house shall be called a house of prayer for all nations. . . . But you have made it a den of robbers" (Mk 11:17)? The disciples' minds turned to the words from Psalm 69:9, "Zeal for thy house will consume me" (Jn 2:17).

4. He took care to make his action stick. Once men and animals were driven away, he "would not allow any one to carry anything through the temple" (Mk 11:16). Other translations give the impression that he physically barred the way of anyone else who came to carry on the wretched business.

Now let us be clear about what we are discussing. We are not discussing nonviolence or the pros and cons of passivism. The question is, Did Jesus display anger? We are not even asking whether we have the right to do the same thing. Our only question is, Does the incarnate Word reveal what the written Word in the Old Testament reveals about God's wrath as well as his love?

The glorified Jesus seen by John on Patmos was consistent with all that went before. "I heard a loud voice from the temple telling the seven angels, 'Go and pour out on the earth the seven bowls of the wrath of God' . . . and God remembered great Babylon, to make her drain the cup of the fury of his wrath" (Rev 16:1, 19).

There is no room for doubt. From Genesis to Revelation our God is a God of anger.

The Theological Problem

It is here that I must tread with reverence and care, not because theology is a complex subject we shouldn't discuss without a Ph.D., but because our minds are not great enough to comprehend our God in his glory and majesty.

Let me be as simple as I can.

First, does God have the right to be angry? I know it sounds like a silly question, but it is critical. You say God has the right to do whatever he likes. Does he? Does he have the right to lie? That's an awkward question.

Is righteousness *above* God, so to speak, in that he is subject to its laws? If so, who invented righteousness, and who checks to see that God keeps the rules? Yet if God has the right to do as he pleases and to make all the rules, does not this imply that God has the right to do "wrong"? And therefore may not anger be wrong? You see how mind-boggling such questions are.

The answer is related to the issues raised in chapter one. Is God morally perfect because he keeps all the rules or did he himself give birth to the quality of righteousness which is reflected in the rules? I can only say that God is God and that I have no moral yardstick to measure him with. The nearest I can come to understanding it is to say that God is forever the creator of goodness, that only goodness proceeds from him. Goodness is consistent with and a reflection of his very heart. For the moment I would prefer to leave the matter at that point. I can go no further.

A number of questions arise. God desires that we be made "conformable to his image." Does that mean his anger too? Or does God alone have the right to be angry? He never hints at it in my Bible. We may not often experience it, but there is righteous anger—and there is often justifiable anger.

More important, how do we see God's anger in relation to his other attributes? Does he stop loving when he gets angry? Where do his gentleness and long-suffering go? You know the answers. God is loving *as well as* angry. He is patient and long-suffering *as well as* enraged. How can this be?

To get back to where we started, we can't measure him

by ourselves. We tend to forget to love when we become angry. But God never *becomes* angry. He is, was and will be eternally angry. He is angry with evil and sin. He does not *begin to be* angry with us. It is better to say that when we do evil we walk into that region where his anger already exists, eternally the same.

God's love clearly is more basic than his anger. Scripture says that God is love, yet we never read that God is anger. We might say that his anger arises out of his love. Love and anger come together at Calvary.

You see, anger is the measure of love. Even here on earth we can see that. A normal man is terribly hurt and angry if his wife is unfaithful. If this hurt and angry man loves his wife enough to accept her back, to forgive her and treat her tenderly, then we know he really loves her. On the other hand, if he just shrugs his shoulders at her adultery, we can be pretty sure he doesn't care for her at all. In fact, a man who is never angry is a feeble, shallow, selfish kind of man. He confuses love with emotional goo.

So we must be careful not to think that there is something contradictory about a loving God being angry. God is angry over injustice. He is angry about human suffering and the sin that causes it. He is angry with you when you sin. And the heat of his anger with you is the measure of his love for you. If you reject the idea of his anger, it is because you find his love interferes too much in your personal affairs.

Glad for Anger?

Some people, of course, are glad that God is angry. They remind me of the bratty little girl who came to me one day at school and said, "The teacher's *really mad* at you." You could tell she was just hugging herself with joy. In our witness we aren't called on to play the part of that little girl. God's anger at others isn't something to gloat over. It should move us to fearful concern for them.

On the other hand, we shouldn't avoid the subject. We aren't called to be God's public-relations experts but to be witnesses. The only image we must project is the correct one. We aren't to aim for effect. God's character is not a subject for a media campaign designed to present his best face.

How people react is God's responsibility. And as a matter of fact, people's reactions will depend on the extent to which the Holy Spirit convinces them of the facts we present. Once you are convinced that Mr. Smith is mad at you, your main worry is the fact of his anger. You may resent it. You may fear it. You may feel that Mr. Smith is unjust. But you don't go around arguing that Mr. Smith couldn't be angry because he isn't like that, or that you don't believe in Mr. Smith.

Naturally our witness has to do with other aspects of God and not just with his anger. At times it's a puzzle to know how much to stress any particular aspect. At certain times in history there was less need to stress God's anger because people were already aware of it. We should be guided, then, in deciding how much to stress God's wrath by what people know about him. (Once again, our duty isn't to make either ourselves or God popular, but to let people know what he is like.)

That is, I think, what Jonathan Edwards tried to do when he preached his sermon "Sinners in the Hands of an Angry God." Quite a title. And it must have been quite a sermon if you can go by the people in the church that night. Horror at the thought of God's anger so gripped them that they couldn't move when the preacher stopped. Unutterable anguish for sin rooted them to the floor. And a revival got under way.

Edwards didn't crack a whip, however. He showed no fiery eloquence. If the record is true, he read his sermon in a thin, reedy voice, peering shortsightedly at his manuscript by candlelight. But his idea of God was biblical. And it rang a bell in people's minds because the Holy Spirit was working. It's been said that no one should speak to a non-Christian about God's wrath without tears in his eyes.

The story is told of the "modern" parents who were careful to allow their little girl to express her personality. They never showed anger or disapproval. One day after she had jumped up and down on the grand piano for a while, she paused and asked in frustration, "Won't anything I do make you get mad?" Their indifference had convinced her they did not care.

I'm all for an angry God. Not just because I love him and trust him, but because of what I see in the world around me. Would you want a God who could overlook today's terrorism? The holocausts of concentration camps? The exploitation by commercial enterprises of starving people? The Gulag Archipelago?

His wrath was on Egypt, Assyria, Babylonia, on sinning Israel and Judah. His wrath burns on against iniquity: crime against elderly people in our cities, the persecution of his saints under fascist and Communist regimes, all of the world's torture chambers—everything that exalts itself against him and all he stands for.

I may be wrong, but I feel that individuals and nations are jumping on pianos right now. Among the things that make them do this, I detect a wistful longing to know a God who cares enough to be angry. In the climax of earth's history God's white-hot rage will burn to a clean powder all that is evil and corrupt. We shall live in a new heaven and a new earth—where righteousness reigns.

3
Our Glory
and Our Guilt

_____What is a human being? A complex bundle
of neuron pathways, says the reflexologist. Jab people with
a pin and they jump. Freeze them and they bundle themselves up with clothing and build a fire. Deep inside our
amazing brains are chemical memory patterns that tell us
that these are the appropriate ways to react to pain and
cold. We don't really "think" (though we *think* we "think").
We don't "decide" either. Everything we do is predeter-
mined by stimuli from the environment acting on the complex chemistry of our central nervous systems. "Will,"
"mind" and even "consciousness" are illusions.

What is a human being? A mass of statistical data, says
the statistician. Several million are starving. Several million
others eat too much. The figures for both groups are exploding. But the trends are fascinating, and we've made
great progress in our understanding of humanity since the
advent of the computer.

What is a human being? The highest of the mammals,
says the zoologist. A social animal, declares the anthro-
pologist. The suffering victim of social and family pres-

sures, affirms the psychoanalyst. The victim of the class struggle, says the Communist.

So there you have us—dissected, computerized, reduced to a mass of nervous pathways and overwhelming statistics. But the Bible offers a different picture of us, more different than these explanations are from each other. They have defined us from our behavior; the Bible goes right to our essence. It says we are made in the image of God. The Bible reveals things about humankind that science will never discover. We can only quarrel with those who say "We are this *and nothing more.*" For we are more. Having described our physiology, we are a long way from having said what is most important about us. What the Bible has to say is key. For we can be described not only in terms of the physical universe but also in terms of eternal purpose.

If we want to know what anything *is,* we must ask *what it is for.* What is a bread knife? You could say it is a thin strip of steel, sharpened along one edge, and your statement would be accurate. But if you said nothing more, you'd have said very little. If, on the other hand, you said that a bread knife is something you cut bread with, you'd be getting nearer the heart of the matter.

Therefore, our understanding of humanity will be at best sadly incomplete unless we see what we are for. At this point the Bible can give us only part of the answer, since our minds cannot stretch enough to grasp the whole. Among other things, we were created to enjoy God by knowing him. "Let him who glories glory in this, that he understands and knows me, that I am the LORD" (Jer 9:24). We were also made to please him by knowing him. "I desire . . . the knowledge of God, rather than burnt offerings" (Hos 6:6).

To know him and enjoy him we must in some respects be like him, and have something in us that corresponds to him. We were made in his image—responsible, moral beings (Gen 1:26-27; Ps 8:4-9). If this is so, and if our end is to know God—how great is human dignity! We are more noble than a mere mass of protoplasm, more important than the political creeds we invent, greater than the history we make. We are created to glorify the One who is the God of all time and space.

Sin Now, Pay Later

Our calling, then, is a great one. And what we do with our lives is important. We are responsible creatures. Our actions have consequences that matter eternally. When we fulfill our calling, the results are glorious. When we don't, the outcome is equally momentous. The dignity and worth God has given us mean that our successes are as momentous as our failures.

All our actions have consequences. This is the way the universe operates. If my son throws a ball through the window, either he pays or I do. Should neither of us shell out cash for a new pane of glass, the whole family pays by suffering the inconvenience of a cold and drafty room. The world cannot remain the same, once a ball shatters a pane of glass. You cannot evade the law of consequences.

Nothing in life is free. You may not pay dollars and cents for the air you breathe, but you pay for it by the energy you use to move your diaphragm. Unless you expend that energy, you die. In order to have the energy to expend, you must eat—food that someone has paid for. (Even a mouthful of air can be measured in money!)

The same law operates in the realm of ethics. You can't commit adultery without both paying for it yourself and forcing others to pay too. Even if you and your lover are never caught, you pay in uneasiness, anxiety and a loss of joy in your family.

Moreover, you feel guilty. Guilt means having a sense of the size of the principal that still had to be paid. Your down payment consisted of money, time, anxiety and inner dis-ease. Your guilt feelings are a reminder of that portion of your bill yet needing payment, sometime in the future.

So it goes with any sin, be it pride, anger or dishonesty. Sin is like those commodities you buy on a low down-payment plan. And the longer you go on, the more the bills pile up (as your conscience quickly will tell you). Thus the plan of "sin now, pay later" has the disagreeable result of pitching you into moral bankruptcy before you know it. And pay later you surely will.

Few people, even though they may argue against it intellectually, have any doubt deep in their hearts about this inevitable law. They may hate it. They may even declare it does not exist. Yet, on the deepest level of their existence, they know beyond a shadow of doubt that all of us are responsible for our attitudes and actions. Sometimes, to lessen our anxiety, we juggle the figures in an effort to draw a false, but more comforting, moral balance. We fool ourselves into imagining that we are not so deeply in debt after all. But guilt feelings haunt us still.

One patient who came to me for psychiatric help was more honest. His deepest problem, he told me, was a crushing sense of guilt. How could he overcome it? When I reminded him that he needed to experience forgiveness, he replied, "Yes, but forgiveness implies a forgiver; and to have authority to forgive, the forgiver would have to be of cosmic dimensions. No one else could. And I don't believe in supercosmic beings."

I could not help my patient by leading him into an understanding of the merely psychological origins of his guilt feelings, origins that lay in conflicts with a father-figure in his early childhood. However much insight he might gain into his own psychodynamics, he would never be rid of a guilty conscience. For guilt is real. It corresponds to the nature of reality. Though our sense of guilt may be exaggerated or diminished, our consciences correspond, however faultily, to things as they truly are.

The Cancer and the Pain
We all know what guilt feelings are like. They make us unhappy and anxious. Some people take baths when they feel
guilty. Others bury themselves in a book, or drown their
anxiety in whiskey. Children avoid their parents or sit staring at their plates during mealtime.

But let me be clear. *Guilt feelings* and *guilt* are not the same
thing. No two people share the same standard. What may
seem wrong to you may be approved by your neighbor,
whereas things you can do with a clear conscience might
bother him or her tremendously. The aim of modern psychology is to rid people of guilt *feelings*, at least of those guilt
feelings that prove incapacitating. In contrast, the aim of
the Bible is to teach us how we can be rid of guilt itself, and
what guilt really consists of.

Both approaches have merit, but it must be obvious that
the Bible's approach is incomparably more important. Sin
is to guilt feelings what cancer is to pain. If a man has
cancer, you will do him a great service if you relieve him
of his pain. But if you take away the pain without taking
away the cancer (difficult, but not impossible), you do him
only a partial service. If, on the other hand, you relieve him
of the pain by getting rid of his cancer, you will do him an
even greater service.

But what if you could not convince the person that he in
fact is a victim of cancer? None of us want to be told we have
a malignancy. Happy, therefore, is the person with the
moral courage to take a good look at his inner self to see
whether he is inwardly diseased. The Bible makes it clear
what sin is. Mark 7:21-23 says, "For from within, out of the
heart of man, come evil thoughts, fornication, theft, murder, adultery . . ." Sinful actions spring from sinful hearts.
Romans 1:18-25 tells us that the inner attitude is one of

rebellion against God, a rebellion that makes us trample intellectual honesty underfoot and perverts our every instinct. "For the wrath of God is revealed from heaven against all ungodliness and wickedness of men who by their wickedness suppress the truth. . . . Therefore God gave them up . . . to impurity, to the dishonoring of their bodies . . ." The story of Adam and Eve shows the consequences of sin. We are separated from God and each other. Made for communion with our Creator, we end up without identity, stumbling in the dark (Gen 3:1-24).

God does not merely treat our pain. He removes the disease. He not only soothes our guilty feelings, but redeems us from sin. He takes account of us as whole people and gives us a whole new existence.

Such an approach, as we shall see in chapters five and six, is costly. In God's case it cost the life blood of his Son to deal with our sin. Just as we will never rescue alcoholics from Skid Row unless we deal with their alcoholism, so God can only redeem us to a new way of life by dealing with our guilt. God's redemption goes much further than forgiveness. It entails a rescue from futility and remotivation in a God-ordained way of life. It restores us and empowers us to fulfill our calling to know, to glorify and to enjoy the One who made us to be his own.

4
The Four Travelers

Once upon a time four travelers sat down in a sandbox that, unbeknown to them, was ridden with fleas. The longer they sat, the more uncomfortable they became, until one by one (each suspecting that the rest would not understand), they rose to their feet and went their separate ways.

The first traveler was walking along the forest glade when he saw an old lady who looked as though she might be a witch, though a witch of a superior class. "Good Madam," said he, bowing and scratching, "do you have spells to cure itching?"

"I don't sell spells," the old lady returned gravely, "but it is possible that you have a flea. At the end of this path you will find a river lit by the setting sun. Take off your garments and wash them in it. Then jump in yourself and take a bath. When you are clean, cross the river, not by the bridge but by wading through its deepest part, and put on your clothes on the farther bank."

"Fleas?" thought the first man sensibly as he left the old lady. "Fleas are not very nice to think about. I probably don't have fleas. I'm just imagining things. The best thing I can do is forget about the whole business."

So as he came to the river, he crossed by the bridge with scarcely a downward glance. By and by (he was a strong-minded man) his itching grew less. When last I heard, he was the president of several corporations, housing a whole army of fleas in his underwear but scratching himself only occasionally.

The second traveler followed the highway, but before long he too met the old lady who looked like a witch. "Good Madam," said he, bowing and scratching, "do you have spells to cure itching?"

"I don't sell spells," the old lady returned gravely, "but it is possible that you have a flea. At the end of this path you will find a river lit by the setting sun. Take off your garments and wash them in it. Then jump in yourself and take a bath. When you are clean, cross the river, not by the bridge but by wading through its deepest part, and put on your clothes on the farther bank."

"Fleas?" said the second traveler as he left the old lady behind. "I don't want to offend the old dear, but who after all is entitled to say what is a flea and what is not? The question is purely relative. In my opinion, fleas exist only in the mind. I admit that I itch, but that's because I was inflicted by punitive parents with a belief in hygienic absolutes."

So saying, he too crossed the bridge over the river whose waters flashed red in the sunset. Later in life, as a psycho-analyst, he amassed a great fortune by taking itches seriously. His flea-bitten patients were told that society had burdened them with a flea complex. The road to release was not easy. They must be courageous, defy convention and sit in a sandbox.

The third traveler saw the old lady, but something in the way she looked at him made him itch all the more. So he went the other way and bought a large bottle of pills at the village drug store. The pills gave him a lovely, woozy feeling to help him forget the itch. The last I heard of him, he was a famous movie actor, very flea-bitten and woozy most of the time.

The last traveler discovered he had fleas even before the old lady told him. She found him with his shirt off (he blushed when he saw her), dabbing his torso with the moistened tip of his finger, as one of the fleas hopped nimbly out of his way between his shoulder blades. "I'll never get rid of these things," he told her plaintively.

The old lady smiled. "At the end of this path you will find a river," she told him, "lit by the setting sun. Take off your garments and wash them in it. Then jump in yourself and take a bath. When you are clean, cross the river, not by the bridge but by wading through its deepest part, and put on your clothes on the farther bank."

"Well, there's no harm in trying it," the fourth traveler said. "I'd do anything to get rid of the pests." When he got to the river, he did what the witch had told him, and he rose damp but flealess on the far bank.

Later in life he became a most successful grandfather (far nicer than being a psychoanalyst or a film star), who used to admonish his round-eyed grandchildren with a shake of the finger and the solemn words, "Always get rid of the flea, my dears, and the itch will take care of itself."

5
Christ:
Born of a Virgin

The virgin birth is more than just a Christmas story. It is a fact of history on which salvation depends. No virgin birth, no forgiveness of sins.

In a way it is as vital as the empty tomb. For if the resurrection shows that Jesus is divine, the virgin birth shows that he is also human. And in order to save us, he has to be both.

That may explain why from Jesus' day until now the doctrine of the Incarnation has always been under attack. People have resorted both to superstition and to sneers. The Docetists said that he was never truly human. He was a walking illusion that looked human but was not. There was nothing of Mary's humanity in him. Well, a walking illusion cannot *die*. And only a real death can provide a real salvation.

A Beautiful Myth?
The more common tendency is to say he had a human father. This way he would be human enough, but sinful and not divine. As a sinner, however, he could never offer himself as a sacrifice for sin.

Another theology takes the divinity of Jesus more seriously and attempts to show that though he was born a mere man, he *became* God. The *adoptionist* view advocated by J. A. T. Robinson sees Jesus as being adopted as the Divine Word at his physical resurrection from the dead. We could call it the-man-who-became-God view.[1] But is this what the New Testament teaches? Clearly the answer is no.

Some people say, "Isn't this beautiful myth only one of many myths among early peoples about supernatural births? It is true that the Christian myth is *nicer*, but is it essentially different?"

Yes, it is. It is different not only in content but in its very essence. Ancient myths are of two kinds—the fantastic and the disgusting. The story of Mary's conception is neither.

Take myths that grow up around the birth of Buddha, for instance. One story has it that an elephant entered the left side of a noble Indian lady. Inside her it turned into Buddha. Stripped of poetry and symbolism, and conceived of as a historical event, this story is not just fantastic; it is comic! Whatever you may believe about the story of Mary's conception, it is neither bizarre nor comic.

The Greek legends, on the other hand, are understandable but disgusting. They have to do with gods who had sensual passions and who came down to earth to make love to human women. To suggest that the account in Scripture of what God did to Mary is "only another (but superior) legend" is not only offensive, but it is absurd. For the Holy Spirit was in no sense the natural father of the Lord Jesus. Indeed, this takes us to the very heart of what the Incarnation was and how radically Christ differs from the half-gods of Greek mythology. He was not the product of sexual union, but of a miracle performed in the body of a woman. From Mary he took a complete human nature. He was a whole man—not half-man, half-god.

In the early church, the Docetists were not the only ones

to teach error about Christ. There was Nestorius, for instance, who was so obsessed by the two sides of Christ's personality that he practically made him into two persons. The Son of God and the man Jesus were linked together like Siamese twins. Another teacher, Eutyches, went to the other extreme. He taught that Jesus was one person with one nature.

Perhaps the most ingenious idea was that of Apollinarius. Apollinarius would have fitted well, in some ways, into a modern fundamentalist church. He believed, for one thing, that we are tripartite beings—body, soul and spirit. Jesus, he taught, had the body and soul of a man, but in place of his spirit was the divine being.

The idea at first seems harmless enough. But it is not what the Bible teaches. The real truth is at once simple and deeply mysterious. More than this, in Apollinarius's thinking, God the Son never became truly human. *He merely inhabited the shell of a human personality.* And Scripture teaches plainly that God did not just indwell a human personality. He became man. "Therefore he had to be made like his brethren in every respect . . . to make expiation for the sins of the people" (Heb 2:17).

The Mystery of God and Man

What the Bible really teaches was clarified by the church leaders who met in Chalcedon in the year 451. They did not attempt to lay bare every aspect of the mystery of the Incarnation. What they did do was to establish certain essentials that serve to guide us even today. They declared that Scripture teaches that Christ is one person with two natures —a divine and a human. He is man and he is God; yet he is one Person. He did not become less God by becoming a man. Nor is he less man because he is God. "The Word was God" (Jn 1:1). "The Word became flesh" (Jn 1:14).

Of course, this poses problems. There is the problem of

his intelligence, for instance. How much did Jesus of Nazareth know? If he was one person, was his intelligence finite or infinite? If he had infinite intelligence, he faced life with resources we can never possess. Therefore could he truly be regarded as man?

We can never fully penetrate the depths of this mystery. But it will help us greatly to understand what the Council of Chalcedon meant when they said Christ had two natures.

The word *nature* is confusing. We see it in different ways. We say, "Jack has a vindictive nature." What we mean is that Jack has a vengeful disposition or character. But when we speak of Christ's human nature, we are not saying that he had a human disposition. We are saying that he partook of the very essence of humanity (what the old theologians called human substance). He thus took on himself the essence of humanity without abandoning the essence of deity.

Now the old theologians are insistent on the fact that while these two essences or substances are united in one person, they are not mingled in any way. They speak of a *hypostatic* union. The human nature retains human properties and the divine nature divine properties, but the two sets of properties do not mingle.

It is here indeed that we stand on the banks of mystery. If we ask whether Jesus possessed human intelligence or divine, the answer is that he possessed both. There were times when he spoke or acted as a man. There were times when he spoke and acted as God. There were times when both natures seemed to play their part.

As he faced temptation and trial, he faced them as a man, using only the resources that we are capable of using ourselves. He was subject to all our limitations, save that of sin. As he fought with disease, demons and death, he did so with the power of God. As he hung on the cross, he did so both as man and as God.

Once we grasp the idea of someone who is both man and

God at the same time, we see that there is only one possible way in which he could ever have entered the world. Theoretically God could have invaded the body of another human being. But in that case, he would not have been one person but two. Moreover there would have been the problem of a sinful nature. He had to be sinless.

Or God could have made the earthly Jesus out of the dust of the ground, just as he made the first Adam. But in that case Jesus would not have been a member of *our human race*. He would have been a special creation. We are all sons of Adam. Only a son of Adam could truly be one of us and represent us.

No, there was really only one way in which the God-man could come into being. He had to be conceived by the work of the Holy Ghost in the body of a human woman. In that way, while not ceasing to be God, he became truly a member of our race, like us and belonging to us in every respect except that he had no sin.

In this way he could die for us and take our place. He is the Second Adam who can truly represent us. He was and is one of us.

His having entered the world in this way gives us an enormous advantage. He knows what we feel like. He knows because he went through it. He was tempted in all points as we are, yet without sin (Heb 4:15). That means he would feel the lure of self-pity and self-indulgence. He would know these things, and yet he would put them in their place.

For that very reason he can be touched with the feeling of our infirmities. As we struggle and weep, there is one who has struggled and wept (with strong crying and tears) before us. He can sympathize because he knows. He can help because he conquered.

Therefore I repeat that the virgin birth is not just a beautiful story. It is a fact on which a lot depends.

Go with the Wise Men

In spirit I go with the Wise Men and the shepherds to look and wonder. I see a baby that looks much like any other baby. No halo, no beautiful smile (newborn babies do not smile). No frills or talcum powder either. Just a baby in the swaddling clothes of a peasant. When it is hungry it screws up its little face and cries (I shrink from saying "*He* screws up *his* face and cries.") It has to be fed.

I fall down with the Wise Men and worship. I worship not only because I am in the presence of God but because I am beginning for the first time to see what God is like. And I am overwhelmed. I want to turn my head away for I am appalled at his humiliation. And yet I want to look, for I am glad with all my heart that he has done it. He has become one of us. He has not despised the virgin's womb. He has been born of a woman, made under the Law. He has come to live among us, to suffer and to die.

So I worship. And with my cracked voice, as well as I can, I sing with the hosts who adore him: Glory to God in the highest. Oh, come let us adore him, Christ the Lord.

6
Christ:
Died on a Cross

_____Everything depends on who died.

If all they did was hang a local preacher in a minor Roman province, then we may call it trivial. The fact that it sparked a great religion proves nothing. Even trivia can have vast consequences. The cry of a child can start an avalanche.

But if it was God who was put to death, we can never call the cross trivial. Nothing of greater consequence has ever taken place. Words collapse before the enormity of it. It was the race's blackest, vilest crime and its most hideous and appalling mistake.

Yet, having said that, we have only deepened the mystery. If he was God (and this is what the Bible teaches and what Christians believe), then he must have *wanted* to be crucified. The question is, Why? The answer lies in what is known as the doctrine of the atonement.

I choose the word *doctrine* with care. Some people say the *fact* of Christ's death is vastly more important than how it works. "Let's not quarrel about *how* or *why*," they say. "The great thing is that he died and that this somehow helps us."

I must confess the point impresses me. Obviously, if

Christ achieved something by his death, it is his death (not theories about it) that did so. But I cannot let the matter rest there. Facts owe their value to their meaning. The fact the doorbell rings is only of value to me if I know it means that someone is at the door. If the death of Christ has no meaning, then it has no value.

But the Bible gives us the meaning of Christ's death. At least it gives as much of it as we can grasp. The death of Christ is rarely mentioned in the Bible without some meaning being attached to it. We do not merely read, "Christ died." Rather "Christ died *for our sins*" and *"in accordance with the scriptures"* (1 Cor 15:3). If the doctrine of the atonement represents truth, it does so only insofar as it accurately reflects the Bible's explanation about the meaning of Christ's death.

The Plan of Death

What, then, does the Bible say about his death? It says, for one thing, that it was all part of a plan. He was "the Lamb that was slain from the creation of the world" (Rev 13:8 NIV). It was foreordained. This is important. It is important because some scholars, while admitting that Christ saw his death as inevitable, say he recognized this because circumstances forced him. He had enemies. He was realistic enough to see that the opposition against him had grown too big to beat. He knew when he was licked. So he rose to the occasion. He accepted his fate and turned it into a sublime passion.

There is truth in this, but it is not the whole truth. He did see that he had enemies and he did go (praise his name) as a lamb to the slaughter. But he did not do so because men were too powerful for him. We insist that he is God. If he is God, it is inconceivable that he awoke, too late, to the fact that he was in a jam.

Nor does this idea tie in with other facts. Think, for in-

stance, of what happened at the outset of his public ministry. At his baptism he heard a voice from the skies saying,
"This is my beloved Son, with whom I am well pleased" (Mt
3:17). Beautiful words! But they have overtones our ears
miss. Like the people later on, we hear sounds but fail to
catch the meaning. To Jesus it would be clear enough. A
mind steeped in the Old Testament would know that the
words were a combination of two well-known verses: "You
are my son, today I have begotten you" (Ps 2:7); "My chosen, in whom my soul delights" (Is 42:1).

The first sentence announced him as Son. The second
was taken from one of the "suffering servant" passages in
Isaiah. The voice was telling him not only that he was the
Son but that he was *the* Son who was to suffer. Had he not
known a thing about his mission before this point, he would
have no illusion from then on about its outcome.

The issue had been plainly described in prophecy. As the
Lord Jesus walked with the two disciples on the road to
Emmaus after his resurrection, this is what he stressed.
"Was it not necessary that the Christ should suffer?" he
asked them. "And beginning with Moses and all the prophets, he interpreted to them in all the scriptures the things
concerning himself" (Lk 24:26-27).

The Overcoming Death
Christ's death was foreordained. What did it accomplish?
Two things: Satan's defeat and our redemption. First,
Christ challenged Satan's assumption of power over us and
by a glorious victory overthrew our evil taskmaster to de-
liver us from sin and the grave. Gustav Aulen draws attention to this vital aspect of Christ's death in his classic work
Christus Victor.[1] This conflict with the powers of hell is plainly taught in Scripture and was emphasized by both Eastern
and Western churches during the first eleven centuries
after Christ.

His death was light overcoming darkness, truth overcoming a lie, love overcoming one who had enslaved a race of rebels. How the two aspects, our redemption and Christ's triumph over the powers of hell, fit together is no more easy for our minds to grasp than how God is both the reconciler and the One who is reconciled. Yet Scripture teaches both.

"And you, who were dead in trespasses and the uncircumcision of your flesh, God made alive together with him, having forgiven us all our trespasses, having canceled the bond which stood against us with its legal demands; this he set aside, nailing it to the cross. *He disarmed the principalities and powers and made a public example of them, triumphing over them in him*" (Col 2:13-15). Here is a note of conflict and triumph that permeates the New Testament, particularly noticeable in the book of Revelation.

The Necessary Ransom

The Bible teaches not only that in the death of Christ is found his triumph over Satan. It also teaches that his death was *necessary*. It was to win something that could be won in no other way. This again repels the idea that the Lord was helpless before the Jewish authorities who plotted against him. His enemies were fitting in with his plan. His death was a *must*.

The day Peter blurted out his faith in Christ's divinity, Jesus began to warn the disciples that death lay ahead. Since they knew he was God, he must also make sure they knew his purpose—to die! Peter airily began to take his master to task. Christ's reply startles us by its severity: "Get behind me, Satan! You are a hindrance to me" (Mt 16:23).

Jesus had to die. He was compelled not by circumstances but because there was no other way to do what he came to do. Any voice that sought to deflect him from his course was to Jesus the voice of Satan himself.

When we ask what made that death so necessary, the

Bible does not mince words. He died to *redeem people* and to *forgive sin*. And since, as we have already seen, his death was a must, we conclude that there was no other way in which he could redeem and forgive. If we were to be forgiven and redeemed, *Christ had to die*.

Jesus himself said so. He did not only say he came "to seek and to save" people. (You can interpret those words several ways.) He came to *redeem* them. He came "to give his life as a ransom for many" (Mk 10:45). But is not that saying the same thing? Not necessarily. Some say that Jesus *saves* us by his death, but they do not think he redeems us. He is Savior. He is not, according to them, redeemer. He saves us, they say, by the beauty of his example. When we realize how great God's love is, it so affects us that we undergo a change. That change constitutes our salvation. Christ's death was necessary as a moving example of God's love. It operates psychologically.

Now Christ's death does indeed touch our hearts. But it does much more.

Profound studies have for years been done on words like *ransom* (redemption). To ransom, in New Testament times, meant to pay a price in order to release or buy back something (or someone) in bondage. In our case we were "in bondage" because of our sin. Sin had put us under a sentence. We were drowning in moral debt. And the Son of man came to give his life to ransom us from that situation. The price he paid was his own life.

That is why we use the word *substitution*. *Our* lives were forfeit: *his* life was laid down in our place. That is no theory. It is what Jesus taught.

At the Last Supper Jesus said something which can never be forgotten. It is at the very heart of Christianity. "This is my blood of the covenant, which is poured out for many for the forgiveness of sins" (Mt 26:28). Bishop Wescott (commenting on another passage) teaches that the significance of shed blood is "the liberation . . . of life . . . so that this life became available for another end."[2] His idea was that Jesus' death is in principle the same as the death of the yellow-haired god who wrestled with Hiawatha. His life was laid down *to be released in a new way.*

At first this seems harmless enough. But once again it is less than the Bible teaches. Jesus states quite clearly that his blood was shed "for the forgiveness of sins." True, it may result in life, but it only does so *because it first results in the forgiveness of sins.* And, as Alan Stibbs points out, in Scripture *blood* "stands not for life released but . . . life laid down in death."[3]

Now of course I am assuming that Jesus actually did say that he came to give his life "a ransom for many" and that his blood was shed "for the forgiveness of sins." Some scholars think that Christians altered the Gospels in later centuries, putting words into Christ's mouth. The idea of his death's being a ransom price to redeem us from sin is, they say, an idea invented by Paul. Since Paul invented it, it "couldn't have been" taught by Jesus. It "must have been" added by someone else. But this is begging the question. It is like when, as a teen-ager, I first arrived in the United States. I did not know the Ford Motor Company was American. After all, it was a British company! Therefore, it "must have been" introduced into the States by Britons!

No, the idea that Christ gave his life as a ransom for us to pardon our debt of sin is not Paul's invention. It is an idea born in the Old Testament, and taught in the Gospels, in the Acts and in all of the New Testament.

The Rage against His Son
Beyond the objections to this biblical view of the atonement lies dislike of what it implies—an angry God who will not gloss over sin. We shrink from the idea that God must be "propitiated" (another biblical word) or "appeased"—es-

pecially by blood. It seems to clash with Christ's idea that God is love. It sickens us.

Well, I have seen people turn green in operating rooms in a hospital too. Until they saw an operation with their own eyes, they did not realize that "drastic ills call for drastic remedies." We need to pause here. We are not dealing with fairy stories. We are dealing with God *as he is* and with sin *as it is*. God is holy; sin, horrible. God's burning anger against sin has nothing in common with the tantrums of heathen deities. As we saw in chapter two, it is a settled, deadly, holy rage against a vile and terrible ill. If we choose to embrace the ill, we will step into the rage.

It is not that he wants to harm us. He longs in utter tenderness to fill us with his love. But he has sworn to scorch the deadly horror; and if we choose to stay with it, he will scorch us too. He could not do less and remain God, for he understands how deadly it is. We understand neither God nor sin. He understands both, and his answer is Calvary.

The rage (we cover our faces) burned against his beloved Son. He was made sin who knew no sin, so that we might be made the righteousness of God in him (2 Cor 5:21). Darkness covered the face of the earth—a darkness thick enough to feel. While even the sun hid in shame, Christ was made a curse for us.

Bearing shame and scoffing rude,
In my place, condemned, He stood;
Sealed my pardon with His blood;
Hallelujah! what a Savior![4]

It may be shocking. It may be incomprehensible. But it gives us a message to preach. God does not love us with beautiful, holy vagueness, but with a love that staggered under a cross, that was hung between thieves, that met and destroyed death and paid to the full our debt of sin.

Let us worship God and thank him for it! Let us proclaim it to the ends of the earth!

7
Belief in
the Book

_____"When all else fails, read the instructions."
The trouble is that some instructions, especially those for
assembling mail-order kits, are confusing, obscure. Did the
person who wrote the instructions ever assemble the kit
himself? Does he know what he's talking about? How much
can the instruction booklet be trusted?

God-Inspired

The questions differ only in importance from those arising
in our minds when we approach Scripture. Yet, Paul writing to Timothy, made the statement "All scripture is inspired by God" (2 Tim 3:16). Peter expanded this somewhat in his second letter. He said, "No prophecy ever came
by the impulse of man, but men moved by the Holy Spirit
spoke from God" (2 Pet 1:21). In these verses we get both
the simple statement that it was God who inspired the writing of Scripture, and a suggestion (which does not invite
detailed speculation) as to the manner in which the inspiration took place.

Nowadays we use the term *inspiration* loosely. Artists and

poets are "inspired" as they paint and write. When we speak of their inspiration, we are really referring to a psychological state in which either they see with greater clarity or feel more profoundly. Unquestionably those who were used to write Scripture both saw with clarity and felt profoundly, but divine inspiration implies much more. If such a mental condition existed in the case of prophets and apostles, then it was the direct result of the operation of God the Holy Spirit on them. The writers spoke because they were moved by the Holy Ghost.

Of course, it might be claimed that many other Christians and pre-Christian writers down the ages have been inspired by the Holy Spirit. We hope that all Christian preachers who open their lips speak at the Spirit's prompting. But it is evident that the meaning of the inspiration of Scripture goes beyond even this inspiration, so that Christians associate two other terms with their ideas of divine inspiration —inerrancy and infallibility.

What do they mean? Briefly they imply that not only did God the Holy Spirit move men to write the Scriptures, but he so controlled the way they wrote that the revelation has come to us without being marred by the errors or limitations of the human authors.

Unfortunately we do not possess today any of the actual manuscripts written by these men. What we do have are *copies*, which themselves are copies of yet earlier copies. And in the copies (as distinct from the original manuscripts) there *are* errors—small errors, infrequent and unimportant. (It is calculated on a scientific comparison of the documents we do possess that copying errors probably account for approximately one word in four thousand of our modern Bible, and that no important biblical teaching is affected.) For this reason many statements of doctrine, when speaking of the inerrancy of Scripture, are careful to include the expression "as originally given." The inerrancy applies to the original inspiration.

Some Christians ask, "How could they be free from error if the inspiration came through imperfect humans?" I do not know. I could, however, ask the same question of Christ. How could he be truly free from sin if he was born of a woman whose life, however good, contained sin? For myself I only know *what God did*. I do not know *how he did it*. He gave us a living Word free from sin, and a written Word free from error.

Much speculation has indeed taken place about *how* the Bible was inspired. There are those who explain away the difficulty by saying that the control God had over the writers was rigid. Their minds and emotions played little part. It was as though God were dictating to human secretaries who wrote down word for word what he dictated.

We must, however, be careful not to go further than the Scriptures themselves go. It is true that some passages of the Bible could be regarded as "dictated" (for example, the letters to the seven churches in Revelation 2—3). But it is equally evident that the vast bulk of Scripture is as truly human as it is truly divine. The emotions and the thoughts the writers express are their own. The fact that God inspired these thoughts by his Holy Spirit and guided the way in which they were expressed does not make them any less human. The mystery of inspired Scripture is no different from the mystery of the incarnate Christ. Both it and he exemplify divine perfection while being fully human.

Thus, while we may feel free to speak of "verbal inspiration" (since an inspired Bible will imply inspired words), we must beware of too mechanical a concept of the manner in which that inspiration took place.

Another idea that Christians insist on when they say that the Bible is inspired is the idea of *sufficiency*. There is no place for adding to what God has revealed. We do not need more than the Bible actually gives.

In some places the Bible itself roundly condemns any such additions. In the Apocalypse, John writes, "I warn every one who hears the words of the prophecy of this book: if any one adds to them, God will add to him the plagues described in this book, and if any one takes away from the words of the book of this prophecy, God will take away his share in the tree of life and in the holy city, which are described in this book" (Rev 22:18-19). The Word of God is complete. It needs no additions and will tolerate no subtractions.

The Authority of the Book

From all of this it necessarily follows that the Bible is an authoritative book, authoritative in two senses. It has authority to control our actions just as the police have authority which gives them the right to stop our car when we are speeding or to take us into custody when we are behaving badly in public.

But it also has, as I have already pointed out, the kind of authority that can give us a reliable answer to our questions. We speak of one of our friends as "an authority on music" and of another as "an authority on politics." What we mean in both cases is that our friends have studied so much in these fields that we can go to them confidently expecting a reliable answer to any questions we have. The Bible in the same way can be counted on to give us an utterly reliable answer on any question we have about spiritual matters.

Not all Christians accept this view. Harold DeWolf once wrote, "The authority of the Word of God resides precisely in those teachings by which God now speaks to the living faith of the reader." This somewhat involved sentence seems to mean that those parts of Scripture that become vivid and significant, as I read them, have authority. A clearer statement by William Hordern appears in the same book. "The Bible is an imperfect instrument pointing to the

Word of God." Here is a somewhat different view. By *the Word of God* he means Christ. The Bible is an imperfect instrument through which Christ, who is God's Word to us, is revealed.

Both these views have one thing in common. They imply that I can no longer go with confidence to the Bible, expecting the Holy Spirit to answer my problems simply by illuminating the truth of its pages. If, for instance, the Bible is an *imperfect* instrument, then somehow I must have help in knowing *how* and *where* it is imperfect. An imperfect signpost (even though it is supposed to point to a perfect road) is of no help to me unless I have some criterion by which I can judge *which way it is supposed to point*. I may miss the perfect road because of the imperfections of the signpost. This, in fact, is what actually happens to those who hold such a view.

We know this because as we compare the conclusions they arrive at from their study of the Scripture we find important differences. In part it is because they have disagreed *as to where the signpost is wrong*. This is only natural, for the criterion they have used if traced back far enough is either their own understanding or else their own subjective feeling. What they are saying is simply "I feel sure that the signpost *ought* to point *that* way."

And what if my mind reaches different conclusions from my neighbor's? Who is to say which of us is right? Yet if I regard the Bible as an imperfect instrument and not in itself the Word of God, I must necessarily depend on my own intelligence or else my own subjective impressions to decide which parts of it are trustworthy and which parts are not.

Over against these views come the clear statements of Jesus Christ himself. There is no suggestion of any imperfection when he speaks of the Old Testament Scriptures: "Think not that I have come to destroy the law and the prophets; I have come not to abolish them but to fulfill them. For truly, I say to you, till heaven and earth pass away, not an iota, not a dot, will pass from the law until all is accomplished" (Mt 5:17-18).

Logically, of course, there are only two other possible authorities for Christians, if the Bible itself is not our final court of appeal. We must turn either to some human being or to some human institution (such as the papacy). If someone such as the Pope represents final authority, then either he must possess intelligence that is very much greater than that of other human beings or else by some miracle he must be gifted with the powers of making infallible pronouncements.

Yet some think that holding the Bible itself as authoritative is bibliolatry. It gives the Bible a more exalted position than Christ's. Christ is the authority! He is Lord! Nothing and nobody, not even the Bible, must be allowed to take his place!

But surely there is confused thinking here. First, there are grades of authority. There is what we might call *final authority* and there is *derived authority*. In a democracy final authority (in theory at least!) rests with the people. The president possesses derived authority—authority delegated to him by the popular will of those who elected him.

Final authority in the cosmos rests with God the Father. The authority even of the Son is derived from him. The Bible too, even though it has authority over our lives, possesses only derived authority, authority derived from God himself. We obey it because it is the Word *of God*. When we subject ourselves to the Bible, it is not really the Bible we are obeying, but the One who inspired the Bible. To set up the Bible as an independent authority would indeed be sin, but this is not what we mean when we speak of the absolute authority the Bible possesses.

Second, the accusation of bibliolatry implies that there is some kind of conflict between the Scriptures and Christ, between what they teach and what he teaches, between what they want us to do and what he wants us to do. Nothing could be more absurd. Jesus himself was most anxious to underline this. He did not come to destroy the law but to fulfill it.

Indeed our very insistence on the lordship of Christ must affect our attitude to the Bible. The authority of Jesus, like the authority of the Bible, must be over both our minds (what we think) and our wills (how we behave). If he is a fallible authority who must be consulted with caution about divine things because his answers may contain human errors, then it will be a dangerous matter to commit our destiny into his keeping.

The opinion that Christ had about Scripture is clear. In his recorded teachings, he refers to twenty different Old Testament characters and makes quotations from nineteen different books. After his resurrection he said to his puzzled disciples, "O foolish men, and slow of heart to believe all that the prophets have spoken" (Lk 24:25). It was Christ who asked almost derisively, "Have you not read . . . ?" (Lk 6:3). It was he who said, "It is written . . ." (Lk 4:4), "Scripture cannot be broken" (Jn 10:35), and, "The scriptures . . . bear witness to me" (Jn 5:39). If we accept the authority of Christ, we must accept the authority of Scripture.

It is true, nonetheless, that even Christians who agree the Bible is authoritative and inspired may differ as to what it means. Doctrinal differences arise among those who trust Scripture and sincerely depend on the Holy Spirit. Why?

Understanding Scripture involves lifelong learning. We wear spectacles when we read, spectacles of bias, of cultural prejudice, of all we have ever learned before. We unconsciously say, "This sentence *must* mean this," unaware of the presuppositions we bring to the text. Learning involves a progressive shedding of the false lenses we have acquired over the years.

Testimonies to the Word

Why accept the Bible as the Word of God? Of the many reasons we have already mentioned, two stand out: that it seems the only reasonable answer to the problem of authority and that Christ himself apparently accepted its reliability and authority. Many of us in actual fact accept the Scriptures for the simple reason that they have spoken so powerfully and overwhelmingly to our own hearts. But other profound reasons should be briefly mentioned.

The Bible is a unity. If by some magical powers we could call together a score of writers from different countries belonging to different ages and ask them to write their views about God and about the things that are most important in life, it would be surprising if their writings harmonized into a perfectly blended symposium. Yet without the least possibility of collusion, the biblical writings are startlingly one in their message and in their advice about how we should live. It is too bewildering a coincidence to be accounted for in any way other than by the explanation given by the Bible itself—divine inspiration.

Then there is the matter of prophecy. Recall the remarkable way in which many prophecies, especially those which foretold details of the life and death of Christ, were so perfectly fulfilled. More convincing evidence of the authenticity of the Bible could hardly be imagined.

Less important but still striking is the growing volume of evidence from archaeology and the new linguistic sciences. As the secrets of ancient civilizations are uncovered by the archaeologist's spade, and as scientific linguistics decode the writings of bygone civilizations, confirmation piles on confirmation testifying both to the accuracy of the Scriptures and to their early dating.

Most convincing of all is the effect of these writings on the lives of those who take them seriously. An atheist once publicly challenged Harry Ironside of Chicago to a debate on their respective beliefs. Dr. Ironside accepted the challenge but proposed that his opponent bring to the meeting a hundred persons whose lives had been revolutionized for the better by atheism. The atheist could not. Dr. Ironside then stipulated that ten people only were necessary. For himself, he promised to bring ten Christians whose lives had been delivered from drunkenness, lying and pride by the Word of God. In the end the poor atheist had to confess that he could not produce even one person and gave up the debate. No more eloquent testimony to the claims of Scripture could be found than the lives of those who read it.

How can we convince others of our position? There is no need to do so. While we should always be ready to explain why we believe that the Bible is the Word of God, divinely inspired, there is little point in laboring to convince our friends of this. They must find out for themselves.

Dr. Spurgeon, the well-known preacher, said that to defend the Bible is like defending a caged lion. It is foolish, he pointed out, to stand outside the cage with a drawn sword to protect the lion from its attackers. The most effective way to defend the lion would be to open the cage and release it. The Bible, like the lion, is well able to look after itself. The best way to convince people that it is the Word of God is to encourage them to read it for themselves with an open mind.

The same applies, of course, to us. I have not written this to remove your doubts about whether the Bible is truly the Word of God. If you want to be convinced of the truth of what I am saying, do not study what I have written. Take down your Bible and read it. Read it prayerfully. Read it carefully. And, above all, read it with a willingness to put it into practice.

You will find that instead of mastering it, it will master you. Such is the power of the Word of the living God.

8
Doctrines
and Divisions

_____Sometimes we hear that doctrine causes divisions. The implication seems to be that we should place less emphasis on doctrine for the sake of unity among Christians.

But can real unity ever exist at the expense of truth? Some doctrines certainly are more important than others. But which doctrines are these? By what criteria do I judge the importance of a given doctrine?

It was Jude, writing in the first century, who asserted that Christians should "contend for the faith which was once for all delivered to the saints" (v. 3). The words are significant. They sum up perfectly the proper attitude of Christians toward doctrine down the ages, and they explain as we examine them the reason for that attitude. We must ask ourselves, What did Jude mean by "the faith"? Why should we "contend" for it? What does the expression "once for all delivered" mean? And, who are "the saints"?

The Need for Creeds
The Faith. The word *faith* is understood by Christians in two

ways. *Faith* can mean an attitude of our hearts toward God. In this sense we *exercise* faith. But *faith* is also used in the Bible to describe what we believe. Jude here speaks of "the faith," not in the sense of the attitude of the soul of the Christian but in relation to the content of that faith—the doctrines that compose it.

Perhaps the first thing to notice about this faith, however, is that it is described by Jude as a given faith. It is a faith that had been delivered (Greek: "handed over to, placed into the care of, entrusted to") certain people.

At once the question arises: Given by whom? The Scriptures answer that it is a body of truth given by God. It is *revealed* truth. Truth that we could not have known in any other way had God not revealed it and entrusted it to us.

It is impossible to exaggerate the importance of the fact that biblical doctrines are *revealed* doctrines, for revelation places them in a category which differs from every other form of human knowledge. As mentioned in the last chapter, if as human beings we are to have a knowledge which is both universal and totally reliable, that knowledge has to originate outside ourselves. It cannot be the product of our limited, fallible minds, or of our fallible and finite observations.

If we had invented the truth ourselves, then any authoritative proclamation of it would be presumptuous. We might be entitled to explain views of our own as our firmly held opinions, but we could hardly proclaim them as divine truth unless God had indeed taken pity on our frailty and our naiveté, and shown us things we never could have known apart from his kindness in showing them to us.

We can take no credit for revelation. It was not given to us because we deserved it either morally or intellectually. For God to give us any truth is an expression of his grace. Therefore, any arrogance about our possessing revealed truth is sinful and offensive to God. But without revelation there is no hope for certain knowledge. If we are to be sure that God exists, and to know what he is like and what he demands of us, *he himself has to tell us.* We cannot, have not ever, will not ever find him by our unaided search.

Some Christians I meet seem strongly opposed to statements of doctrine. They say that the Christian revelation is too great to be reduced into mechanical formulas. This is true. Yet for two millenniums the church has found creeds and confessions necessary. Can we so lightly brush aside two thousand years of history? Although no human words can adequately express divine revelation, is the alternative to leave the matter completely in the air?

What is the purpose of a doctrinal confession anyway? Obviously it is not to explain the whole truth of God. (The Bible itself does so, at least as far as it is possible within the limitations of our finite minds.) Evidently our forefathers keenly felt the necessity of emphasizing what they considered to be certain vital features of the divine revelation, certain elements which under no circumstances must be neglected or perverted. They seemed impelled to re-express in the language of their day the essentials of the evangel. Why?

The emphasis on doctrine and doctrinal statements goes back to the dawn of Christian history. While they were used in later times in the liturgical worship of the church, their original function seems to have been twofold. They were used first of all as a basis for the reception of new members into the church. They were also used to guard the church from error.

So it was that when the eunuch asked Philip under the burning desert skies, "What is to prevent my being baptized?" Philip replied, "If you believe with all your heart, you may." And the eunuch in turn confessed, "I believe that Jesus Christ is the Son of God" (Acts 8:36-37). We have here perhaps the earliest recorded confession of doctrine for admission into the visible church. But the question arises at once: Is not membership in the church based on a new life that the believer has received and not on his understanding of doctrine? *Life* is surely of more importance than *light*.

The answer is that the Bible does not separate the two: Life is dependent on light. If our earth were to lose the light of the sun, within a very short time all life would disappear. Some understanding, however imperfect, of doctrine was the seed that produced life in the believer's heart. Truth and life walk hand in hand.

A famous French preacher once said, "Purity of heart and of life is more important than a correct opinion." To this another French preacher replied, "The cure is more important than the remedy, but without the remedy the cure will not take place." As theologian Augustus Strong expressed it, "A defective understanding of the truth results sooner or later in defects of organization, of operation, and of life. A complete and entire understanding of the truth provides in the first place a valiant defense against heresy and immorality and in the second place serves as a stimulus for the conversion of the world."

Thus, while doctrine can never be a substitute for spiritual life, the early churches quickly saw that without a minimum of understanding, life would not be present. Without light there is no life.

More important than their role in receiving new members into the church, doctrinal statements in the Bible guarded against error in the early church. The letters of Paul battled against Jewish legalism. The letters of John attacked errors about the person of Christ. James opposed what later became known as antinomianism. The Nicene Creed, formulated in A.D. 325, asserted that Christ was truly God, in opposition to the errors taught by Arius. In the year 381 another creed from Constantinople opposed the doctrines of Apollinarius, asserting that Christ was also truly man. From Ephesus in the year 431 came statements designed to combat the false teachings of Nestorius, and from Chalcedon in 451 came a yet more carefully worded statement to counteract the heresies of Eutyches. With the Reformation longer and more complete articles of confession, opposing Roman doctrines, came into being: those prepared by Luther, the catechisms, the famous confession of Augsburg, and the like.

To sum up, doctrine is a means to an end—the end of producing a spiritually alive, spiritually healthy, truly witnessing church. The end is more important than the means, but without the means the end cannot be gained. There never has been and there never will be life, health and vigor in a church steeped in error. It is for this reason that both history and (more important) the Bible are insistent that we should contend earnestly for the faith.

A Fear of Fanaticism

Contend. The word disturbs us a little. Doctrine is important; but must we *fight* for it? As we think of the problems in the church today, the struggles within and the threats from without, we must ask ourselves honestly: Is this a time for striving? Yet the elements of today's issues are no different from those of the crises of the first century. God speaks to us now as he did then, inciting us to contend earnestly.

Paul, writing to the Galatians, felt so keenly the desperate importance of this matter that he cried, "But even if we, or an angel from heaven, should preach to you a gospel contrary to that which we preached to you, let him be accursed" (1:8). Elsewhere he advises Timothy to "take heed to yourself and to your teaching" (1 Tim 4:16).

We must, of course, be careful to understand what New Testament writers meant when they wrote about contending. They were not urging us to lose our temper because someone disagrees with our opinions. Nor were they telling us to use doctrine, even correct doctrine, as a kind of weapon to attack our enemies with. We do not throw the Bible at the heads of people we do not like! The only enemy whom we should attack with the weapon of correct doctrine is the Enemy of all of our souls. What then does it mean to contend for the faith? It means to publish the truth. Truth is given to be spread abroad. We do not light a candle and put it under a basket, but we put it where it will give light to the whole house. If we have truth, we must proclaim it.

We should have no fear of dealing thoroughly with disputed points. Indeed, if correct doctrine is being undermined, it is all the more reason to emphasize it. Error is our enemy and error must be attacked. This is best done by announcing and explaining the truth. It is never to be carried out to prove ourselves superior to others and certainly never to promote unnecessary divisions in the body of Christ. Most important of all, we must sow the seed of truth in the hearts of all new believers.

But if we do this, will we not inevitably cause division, however kindly we do so and however fine our motives? That depends on the reaction of our hearers, but it must be admitted—sometimes, yes. People do not always like truth. Paul himself indicated that at times division within the church was necessary, that the truth and those who adhered to it might be made evident (1 Cor 11:19). After all, unity must not be based on error. Therefore, though we must not strive to cause divisions, we must not allow a fear of division to cause us to compromise the truth.

Basically, the word that causes us the most trouble is *ardently*. It suggests fanaticism, and if there is one thing we dread, it is to be accused of being fanatics. Yet if truth is so vital, and if what we have is a revelation from God, the only source of life, does it not merit a little fanaticism? Do we not in effect need *more* fanaticism and not *less* in the church?

After all, there is nothing wrong with a fanatic who has the truth! It is a fanatic who is *unbalanced and in error* that we must fear.

Fanatics are people who conquer the world either for error or for truth. Let us be fanatics for truth—let us contend earnestly! As we bring God's message to a fallen world, we are sounding a trumpet of warning and of hope. It is terribly important that the trumpet give a clear and not an uncertain sound. The church is in danger of infiltration, as Jude himself goes on to point out, by teachers of error. A sentimental desire to avoid unpleasant problems must never seal our lips or cause us to "play fast and loose" with the truth.

The trouble is, of course, that some people lack a sense of proportion. They contend for trifles. Yet what may seem trifles to me are obviously not trifles to them—or they would not contend so fiercely.

Who then is to say what constitutes a trifle and what truly is basic doctrine? By what criterion can we distinguish major from minor truth? *Any doctrine that materially affects the saving message that the church preaches is of major importance.* Of prime importance therefore are those doctrines that answer such questions as these: Who and what is God? Who and what are we? What is sin? Who and what is Christ? Where did he come from and how did he enter the world? What is the precise meaning of his earthly life and death on a cross? Is it true that he literally rose (physically) from the dead? In particular, what does God demand of me, and how can my relationship with him be put right? Where can I find an authoritative answer to these questions? Does the Bible provide an answer?

These matters, which I have tried to deal with clearly in this book, are of overwhelming importance. If God has given us answers to these questions, then the answers are worth contending for—to the point of fanaticism if need be.

Breaking the Silence

Once for All Delivered. In every branch of human knowledge there is development and change. What we believe today about the universe is quite different from what we believed yesterday. Galileo was a great scientist, but now we smile a little at his naiveté. And today's beliefs will be smiled at tomorrow. Is it not then to be expected that there will be development in our understanding of the Christian faith? Ought we not to have a different concept of divine truth from that of Christians in the first century? And will not our present doctrines seem inadequate tomorrow?

The answer to these questions lies in the profound difference between our knowledge of God and any other kind of human knowledge. Our knowledge of God, as mentioned above, is by revelation. Not only so, but, as Jude points out, it is a revelation "once for all delivered." Had we developed our own ideas about God, then change could be expected. But if Christian truth is a divine revelation, it needs neither modification nor development. And obviously our knowledge of God can come to us only by revelation.

We have always recognized that *we cannot know what an infinite God is like unless he breaks the silence and reveals himself to us.* And God has spoken. He has spoken by prophets and also by his Son. Paul said that he did not receive his gospel from any human source (Gal 1:11-12). The reason for change and development in other branches of knowledge is that human knowledge, being imperfect, is therefore capable of improvement. But it would be foolish to suppose that we can improve on God's revelation.

Yet throughout the centuries of the history of the church, men and women have sought to adapt and to change Christian revelation. Why? Among the many reasons three can be mentioned: an inadequate acquaintance with the Bible, a wrong attitude before God and an inferiority complex in the face of the philosophies of the day.

The Bible is its own interpreter. The distinction between what the Bible teaches and my interpretation of what the Bible teaches is valid but can be overemphasized. God has assured us that as we study it, looking to him for guidance, his Spirit will lead us into an understanding of truth. We need, however, a correct attitude before him. If we want to do God's will, we will know whether a certain teaching is from God (Jn 7:17).

Yet so often the issue is obscured because theologians down the centuries have been too dazzled by the philosophies that were fashionable in their day, too anxious to impress the current leaders of thought. It was Hardy who, in his article "The Faith, Theology and the Creeds" in *The Christology of the Later Fathers,* wrote of the contemporaries of Arius, "They gave themselves to the task (always delicate and sometimes dangerous) of orienting the Gospel to the best thought of their day. And they may well have thought that the new opportunities that presented themselves to the Christian preacher demanded a declaration of Christian truths in terms that could be understood by that day."

The philosophy then in vogue, Neo-Platonism, conceived of God as being too infinitely removed from our frail humanity for us to be able to have true contact with him. So Arius's Christ became a strange hybrid character—half-divine, half-human, but not truly either. Theology had bowed to philosophy; and theology which bows to a philosophy must always become dated the moment that particular philosophy ceases to hold the center of the stage.

Is it not true that his fascination for Aristotle accounts for some of the erroneous views of St. Thomas Aquinas? Likewise there is a profound influence of existentialism on neo-orthodox theology. As W. Graham Scroggie said, "The garb of truth will change inevitably from one generation to another, but the Truth itself remains the same. The terms in which the redeeming revelation is expressed should be adapted to the prevailing mood of thought of each generation, but the revelation itself can never be influenced either by intellectual fashions or by spiritual fluctuations. Our obligation is not to create a message, but simply to interpret it, to communicate it and to be examples of it." The tragedy is that so many who say they are reinterpreting are actually changing its content.

Ordinary People

. . . to the Saints. We know what Jude meant when he spoke of the saints. They did not wear halos, nor were they distinguished from their brethren by any special sanctity. They were the ones who had been called to salvation. They were the ordinary Christians who made up the church. Among them were many ignorant and unlettered men and women. It is surprising and humbling that the great and unfathomable revelation should have been made to such simple souls. "I thank thee, Father," the Lord Jesus on one occasion said, "that thou hast . . . revealed [these things] to babes" (Mt 11:25).

This is a forgotten lesson. We are too quick to be influenced by the teaching of people who by their own confession are not Christians in the New Testament sense. We should, of course, respect learning and we must never be obscurantists. But it is significant that Jude should point out, as did his Master, that the revelation was given to *saints*, not to universities, not to the best thinkers of the day.

We need be neither surprised nor alarmed if these (the best universities and the best thinkers) do not agree with God's revelation. Great as their wisdom is, they are capable only of producing something that will change with time.

To us has been given a divine revelation. It is the one thing certain in the midst of change, the sure Word which stands as a rock above the shifting sands of changing thought. Let us pay heed to it. Let us contend for it ardently.

Part II
Christian
Witness

9
Is Witnessing Brainwashing?

_____In the early days of the revolution in China, many Christians were shaken by the uncanny similarities between Communist and Christian indoctrination. Mass youth rallies rang with joyful singing. When the atmosphere was "right," testimonies from Communist converts radiated the joy and purpose their new faith had brought them. Dynamic preachers swept audiences along with torrents of irresistible Mao-speak. Sacrifice was called for. Appeals were made. Specially trained counselors dealt with interested inquirers. And Chinese men and women went through an experience which seemed weirdly to ape Christian conversion, at least outwardly.

More recently, many Christians have experienced dejà vu as they have seen hundreds of cults populating the countryside. And they have been jolted by what they have seen. Unfortunately, the phenomenon of conversion was for them the great rock on which their faith rested. Having seen hundreds of people turn to God in response to gospel preaching, they *knew*, or thought they knew, that the gospel was true; yet if a Moonie or a Krishna or any cult member was converted to his or her cult in the same way, by the same methods and with the same psychological results (joy, peace, new zeal) as someone who was converted to Christ, what could this mean?

It means simply that conversion is a psychological phenomenon. People or events can be behind it as easily as the Holy Spirit.

Psychological Conversion

Please don't be alarmed by my statement. The term *psychological phenomenon* simply means something that has to do with the mind and that can be observed. Conversion is a change of mind accompanied by a change of behavior (and therefore it is observable). So when I say that something is a psychological phenomenon, I am not *explaining* conversion but describing it. The big question is, How is it produced and by whom? Minds can be manipulated. Conversions can be manmade. There are techniques for making people so unbearably anxious and confused that a cataclysmic (and little understood) shock tosses every one of their ideas into a new and strangely harmonious relationship. Demagogues use such techniques. Psychiatrists use them. Preachers use them.

Our minds are subject to certain laws and they are, to a limited degree, open to manipulation. If in a large crowd you make me laugh, then cry, then laugh, then cry again; and if you alternately berate and comfort me; and if in addition you repeat certain phrases insistently: if you do these things to me, then my mind, if I am not on my guard, will become increasingly like putty in your hands.

There may come a point in which you can do what you like with me. My judgment is impaired, my conscience is inflamed, my emotions make everything seem different. If in such a condition I make the decision you want me to make, whatever that "decision" may be, I will probably experience relief, joy and peace. This is a well-known psychological phenomenon. The techniques for demonstrating it are equally well known. Even if I am on my guard they may be hard to resist, at least temporarily.

The truth of Christianity, however, does not rest on the fact that Christians have been converted to it. We are sure that Jesus is God and Savior because God raised him from the dead. So our faith rests on a historical fact, not on a psychological phenomenon.

Also, while *some* Christian "conversions" have a merely human origin, not all do. The genuine Christian conversion is accompanied by something that God does within a person. It is accompanied by spiritual as well as psychological changes, and by a progressive change of character as well as by a redirection of enthusiasms. In spiritual conversion the emotional changes are the results of God's working, for he gives rise to all the fruits of righteousness. In a purely psychological conversion they result from a technique or from emotional pressure. They do not represent a miracle of grace.

If we preach the gospel, then we must know what we are doing. We must be on our guard against using our skills to perform mass psychotherapy. We are collaborating with the Holy Spirit. We shouldn't be so intent on getting big numbers of conversions that we take over his job. Our role is to explain God's Word *in the power of the Holy Spirit* and to point out how it applies. His work is to make the Word so stick in people's consciences that they come under conviction. We should not play on the minds of people by telling awesome stories. The Holy Spirit will do the convicting and the awakening of fear. Stories are to illustrate obscure points, not to give our listeners the creeps.

Does this mean that all evangelistic techniques are wrong?

No, I don't think so. It is impossible to do anything without some kind of technique. We need technique to communicate truth clearly. I would rather say that techniques *become* immoral when either consciously or unconsciously we use them *to tamper with the will, emotions or conscience of another person.* They also become immoral when they assume more importance in our thinking than the Spirit of God. They become immoral when results matter more to us than people do.

False Emotion

I am not against emotion in preaching, but I am against emotional*ism*. I am not against earnest persuasion, but I am against using tricks to make people change their minds. Paul pleaded with men and women, weeping as he pleaded. This is magnificent. The gospel of Jesus Christ is not a cold, intellectual proposition any more than the plight of a Christless man or woman is a matter of mere academic interest.

So let us have tears but not "tear-jerkers"; and pleading but not persuasion techniques. (You plead when you're concerned; you use a persuasion technique when you've read a manual on methodology and learn how to get people to make decisions.) I'd far sooner have a weeping preacher and a dry-eyed congregation, than the reverse. Preachers have something to weep about. They see, or should see, things as they are, and it is their job to communicate what they see. They may not be able to control their emotions.

The danger of psychological manipulation does not confine itself to mass rallies, however. Techniques of personal evangelism can be just as dangerous. Ever come across people who tell you, "Oh, I've been through that already"? You questioned them and found that they had "accepted the Lord" when some overzealous Christian pushed too hard. It is true that some such "converts" may represent regenerate men and women who are not walking in obedience. But I am equally certain that many more are the products of evangelistic brainwashing.

Part of our trouble arises from our desperation for results. "Full-time" workers have to prove they are laborers worthy of their hire. They have to get results and are as desperate to do so as a salesman. Christian students prove their Christian maturity (like braves prove their physical prowess) by taking a few scalps.

Now results are admirable. I dare not say we should not be bothered when people around us do not get saved. We should be *very* bothered. But results have to be genuine to be any good. It is regeneration that fits people for heaven, not going through the motions of a psychological conversion.

Again, what about the motive I have in wanting results? Does it spring from concern for my neighbor? Does the love of Christ constrain me? Do I yearn for God's glory? Or am I just trying to prove something?

False Motive

Another problem underlying our passion for results is that we belong to a sales culture. The real representatives of the twentieth century are not scientists or astronauts but sales representatives. They are the ones who really keep the wheels turning. And the success of salesmen is measured by the number of things they can sell.

Many salesmen have doubts about the quality of the product they are selling and are honest enough to share these with their customers. Others, however, repress these doubts and use the techniques they have been schooled in. Indeed, big companies have their own methods for keeping the salesmen's morale at a high pitch.

Salesmen must dress well and drive nice cars. This creates an aura of success, and success breeds success. They must be "interested in" their customers, and their interest must be "genuine." (Yet can any interest be genuine when the ultimate motive is a sale, the commission and the kudos?) Salesmen who succumb to such thinking demonstrate not only the virtue of their products, but that their product is just what their client needs.

Living in a world of door-to-door salesmen and their more sophisticated cousins (television and radio commercials, magazine ads and a thousand-and-one publicity stunts), it is only natural that we should think of the gospel as one more thing to sell. Indeed, many teachers openly state that evangelism is a matter of sales technique.

The comparisons are obvious. We *do* have something the whole world needs. We *are* responsible to get the knowledge of this to every creature. Time *is* important. Men and women *should* be deciding to get what we offer.

But there are dangers in the comparison. Mrs. Smith may (under the salesman's technique) buy brushes and later realize that it was not what she wanted to do at all. She has been, in a mild way, brainwashed. It will be annoying for her, but no great tragedy. It is a far more tragic thing if her decision for Christ represented merely giving way to Christian salesmanship.

False Hope

If the Holy Spirit has not been at work in Mrs. Smith's heart, she is not born again. Her "faith" is not saving faith. She has a false hope.

If, on the other hand, she later reacts against her "conversion," her "sales resistance" against the gospel will increase sharply in the future. All over the world there are vast numbers of people who are doubly on their guard against the truth of Christ because they have passed through a spurious conversion experience.

What's more, the sales concept is full of moral pitfalls. It goes against the very nature of witness. Dress well? Why? To impress? For testimony's sake? Does testimony consist of a sharp suit and ivy-league collars? Or are we confusing testimony with reputation and public image?

Worse still: Are you one of those miserable Christians who is trying to put on a victorious front "to attract people to Christ"? This of course is the spiritual equivalent of the sharp suit. You smile (or you are supposed to) because a Christian is joyful. You try to be Christlike though you have no clear idea of what "Christlikeness" is.

It's part of the technique. You must *attract* people to Christ. And if this means suppressing some of the real you and putting on a big act in public, well, that's part of the testimony. The real you pops out in the bedroom where there is nobody but God to see you. And he doesn't matter for he is not a customer. He's already on the right side.

Is Evangelism Immoral?

Many voices in Christendom are protesting against the kind of desecration of human personality I have been describing. They may not use the word *brainwashing,* but they are talking about the same thing. They ask, What right does anybody have to try to change the sincerely held beliefs of others? How dare we manipulate the minds of others? How can we respect them as human beings and yet tamper with their personalities so that, whether they wish it or not, we make them change their whole outlook on life?

Many people find the answer simple. The Communist and the Nazi and the cult member feel that their "truth" is important enough to justify any method of making people believe it. The Roman Catholic Church has at times openly acted on the same conviction, and I'm quite sure many evangelicals have too. The argument runs like this: People need the truth I have; therefore, I should go to any length to make them accept it.

But just what length constitutes "any length"? History speaks of what this has meant to some: concentration camps, torture chambers, the Inquisition. Yet are any of them, in themselves, more terrible than the operation of tearing someone's soul from its moorings, reshaping it and then handing it back to him? We have no right to play God; he alone has the right to lay his finger on a person's soul.

We certainly do, on the other hand, have a commission to "make disciples of all nations . . . to the close of the age" (Mt 28:19-20). Christians must preach the good news to other "Christians, to White Anglo-Saxon Protestants, to Roman Catholics of every race and color, and also to Chinese, Jews and Blacks, to Eskimos and to Indians, to Buddhists, Muslims, Hindus, Shintoists and to the members of the many sects and cults across the country. Christians are in debt to all people everywhere, and the curse of the ages is on our heads if we fail to pay what we owe. If some, in deploring extreme techniques, are really decrying evangelism, then Christians must refuse to be intimidated.

Dropping such manipulative methods doesn't mean, however, that certain foreign governments will welcome Christian preachers with open arms. What is to me a monumental distinction will be theological hairsplitting to government officials in a Middle Eastern country. If converts are made when I preach the gospel in their country, the officials don't care whether the converts exist because I manipulated their brains or because the Holy Spirit touched their hearts. Whatever the reason, conversions have occurred, and the officials are alarmed. Their pride is offended and, more important, a potential political threat has arisen by the existence of a growing community with a new outlook on life.

But to deplore godly witness because we want to live in a cozy world where no one's feelings get hurt or where no political regimes feel threatened is Christian treason. In the order of things, people are going to be offended by the preaching of the gospel. Although Christians are to be meek and law-abiding, riots and violence have occurred and will yet occur as a result of the gospel's proclamation. Because the delicate political balance may be tilted by a new Christian community, a political regime may be destroyed. Yet none of these possibilities should ever deter a Christian from evangelism.

Whether to evangelize is not in question. We must. So in the next chapter we move on to discuss how our evangelism can be godly.

10
We Are
the Light

In the last chapter I did not define evangelism. Rather I described what it is not and insisted that Christianity without evangelism is inconceivable. But if evangelism is not the same as brainwashing by evangelists, what is it? What is the precise nature of our responsibility to the world, as Christians, regarding the teaching God has entrusted to us?

First, evangelism means *to teach*, to instruct by explaining the content of Scripture (Mt 28:20). Levites in Nehemiah's day "read from the book, from the law of God, clearly; and they gave the sense, so that the people understood the reading" (Neh 8:8). They didn't harangue the people to swallow vaguely understood texts and clichés. Priscilla and Aquila "expounded to [Apollos] the way of God more accurately" (Acts 18:26). Evangelism begins with conveying biblical ideas clearly and relevantly, without any attempt to employ psychological tricks. "We use no clever tricks, no dishonest manipulation of the Word of God. We speak the plain truth and so commend ourselves to every man's conscience in the sight of God," wrote Paul (2 Cor 4:2 Phillips).

Second, evangelism means *to demonstrate* God's power. That power may be revealed by how much listeners are appalled by their sin. It has also, in Scripture, in church history and even today, been revealed by the miraculous. We may find this hard to accept because of our Westernized, rationalist world view. Christians differ over whether the miraculous has any place in evangelism, yet our differences may have more to do with our cultural heritage than with our theology. Sometimes our theology is a rationalization of our culturally acquired way of thinking.

Yet if the power of Satan is being challenged by the gospel, a power struggle is inevitable. That power struggle may become overt in a conflict with demonization, sickness and death, or merely human opposition. "My speech and my message were not in plausible words of wisdom, but in demonstration of the Spirit and of power" wrote Paul (1 Cor 2:4).

Third, evangelism is *to witness*. To witness is to bear testimony to what one has seen, heard or experienced. The apostles frequently bore witness to the resurrection of Jesus from the dead, and modern Christians likewise can declare, "You ask me how I know he lives? He lives within my heart." Witness alone is not evangelism any more than teaching alone is. Yet without it evangelism is incomplete.

Christians must beware, however, of spurious witness. A good witness tells the truth, and to pretend to be victorious when one is not victorious is to live a lie. To pretend during discussion that we know more than we really do is to act a lie. And liars are false witnesses. Jesus told his followers to *let* their light shine (Mt 5:16), that is, to let what they really were (including God's new light within them) become apparent to all. As a witness, Christians are to be open books in which others can read both human frailty and the operation of divine grace.

Fourth, evangelism means *to argue*. Some say argument

gets you nowhere. But Paul argued. "He argued in the synagogue with the Jews and the devout persons" (Acts 17:17). We must be careful, of course. Many an argument is born of pride, and none of us likes to have gentle scorn poured on our statements. So don't confuse argument (of the New Testament kind) with letting people get under your skin, with anger or with a stubborn determination to get the last word in.

By argument I mean firmly, congenially dealing with errors in someone's thinking. I don't wish to imply that it's our duty to demolish all their erroneous thinking. We are not called on to show people what fools they are. And if our approach is right, we will be prepared to admit any errors in our own thinking. The errors in someone else's thinking that should concern us are those that shut out their knowing God. Where we encounter these, we must, like Paul, "destroy arguments and every proud obstacle to the knowledge of God" (2 Cor 10:5).

Watch your motives when you argue. Always be ready to admit it when you are getting out of your depth, but if you see false reasoning blinding a man to truth, challenge his error.

Fifth, evangelism means *to persuade* people. Am I about to contradict all I said previously about violating the personal rights of others? By no means! There is a great difference between earnest persuasion and skillful manipulation.

Manipulators are concerned with results; persuaders (assuming their attitude is truly Christian) are concerned for people. Manipulators grow more efficient as they remain emotionally detached from their victims' personal problems; persuaders are already involved deeply. Manipulators always have an ulterior motive; persuaders need never and should never have one. Persuaders may weep as the person they talk to remains dry-eyed, whereas manipulators are hitting pay dirt when their victim weeps while they themselves remain in full control. Jesus wept over a stonyhearted Jerusalem (Mt 24:37), and Paul "did not cease night or day to admonish every one with tears" (Acts 20:31). True evangelism can never be a cold presentation of facts with a take-it-or-leave-it attitude. My brother may not be a puppet whom I skillfully manipulate, but I remain his keeper. I am to be burdened with my responsibility.

Finally, evangelism means *to "contend for the faith"* (Jude 3). Let me reiterate here a few points that I made at length in chapter eight. We are not called to fight our human opponents. We should not attack those who oppose or misrepresent the gospel. We contend rather with "the god of this world" who blinds the minds of people with error (2 Cor 4:4). We contend against error with truth; therefore, we must publicly assail false ideas. While the main emphasis in evangelism rests on a positive explanation of true ideas, it must include as well a vigorous exposé of error.

Many Christian leaders have gone wrong at this point. Some have made their main emphasis a negative one. Others have publicly expressed the bitter hostility they feel toward people they dislike, thinking they are contending for the faith. Christianity is not served by angry young men —or by angry old men for that matter.

Be aware, however, that once we launch a public assault on error, no matter how charitable our own feelings may be, we will bring wrath down on our heads. No one likes having his or her ideas shown to be wrong. So let those who want everybody to like them, who want to avoid strife and disagreeable situations, avoid Christianity. You can't be a Christian and be universally popular.

Thus far we have considered five aspects of what evangelism is. Now let us look at the kind of people we are to be as we evangelize. The essence of witness is just plain honesty. We *are* salt, whether we feel like it or not. We are not told to *act* like salt but *to be* what we *are*. We *are* light. God has done a work in our lives. We don't have to *try* to shine. We need simply let the light that God put there shine out.

Honest Being
To let my light shine demands no more than honesty. It demands honesty before unbelievers. Witnessing is not putting on a Christian front so as to convince prospective customers. Witnessing is being honest, that is, being true to what God has made me in my speech and in my day-by-day behavior.

Such honesty will demand that we talk about Christ to unbelievers with whom we converse. The fact that we have in the past had to create openings to talk about spiritual things proves that subconsciously we have been avoiding the openings that are continually being presented to us.

We all hide our real selves behind a front. To preserve the image that we create demands that we talk, laugh, behave in a certain way. Our talk is designed to create an impression on people we talk to, build up or preserve the image of ourselves we wish to sell. Now, for many of us, *witnessing* means adding certain Christian features to this image. But in doing so we are preaching ourselves, not Christ.

Real witness, on the other hand, means abolishing the front behind which we hide, not modifying it. To live behind a front is to hide our light. It is falseness; and falseness is opaque to divine light.

Now if we are even partially honest (total honesty is rare and difficult) in a conversation with an unbeliever, we will find it extremely difficult to avoid talking about Christian things. Do you say it is difficult to witness? I maintain that, with a little honesty, it is almost impossible not to witness.

Honest Ignorance
Honesty will demand admitting that we don't know everything. Salesmen are never supposed to be stumped for an-

swers. But we are not called to be salesmen but to be witnesses, that is, to be open about what we know and have experienced.

Are you waiting until you have all the answers before you start to witness? Don't. By all means think through answers to problems, but don't postpone witnessing until you have them all. Be prepared to say you don't know. No one will be surprised. God does not depend on the debating powers of Christians.

Some years ago some Moody Bible Institute students had an evangelistic meeting at the University of Chicago. So intellectual an institution as the University of Chicago had to be intimidating! During a discussion period following their presentation a number of difficult questions were asked. The Moody students had the good sense to admit they couldn't answer some of them.

Their honesty was an integral part of their witness.

And it accomplished its purpose. A University of Chicago faculty member publicly expressed interest in hearing more. He said that for the first time he had met Christians who admitted they didn't know everything. This, he said, far from lessening his confidence in them, had in fact awakened it.

Honest Evaluation

Honesty will also demand the acknowledgment of failure. Failure is bad, but deceit about failure is worse. The end never justifies the means.

I do not mean that honesty means giving way to all our worst instincts. But I do contend that to admit to anger is better than to pretend that we are not angry. I also contend that to admit to failure in our Christian life, far from being prejudicial to testimony, may even be a part of it. Our honesty, of itself, is a witness. It takes spiritual grace and courage to admit failure. Only those who are not concerned about themselves and their public image but about their Lord will be able to do it.

But do not sin and failure put Christ to open shame? Yes, indeed they do. But the shame is not removed by covering sin so much as by dealing with it. And clearly we cannot begin to deal with it until we are honest about it with ourselves and, when necessary, with others.

Don't wait until you are perfect to witness. Witnessing involves being honest all the time—now. Never cover up your weaknesses to witness. What the world is waiting to see is not a perfect Christian but the miracle of grace working in a weak, imperfect Christian.

Many Christians today have a tragic misconception of the importance of the role they play in the conversions of others. We should plead, not because our pleading saves, but because we can't help but plead. We are being true to what the Holy Spirit is doing within us. It is the Holy Spirit who is the real midwife to a newborn soul.

I believe that in modern evangelism, both public and personal, we all too often sell our birthright for a mess of pottage. We think we have harnessed the Holy Ghost when all we have harnessed is cheap psychology. We are not presenting a Person but promoting a symbol. We have been called to the glory and honor of being witnesses to the Lord of history and the redeemer of our race, and we fuss about with our silly techniques for "getting decisions."

It is time we quit our blasphemous fooling. It is time to let our light so shine before people that they glorify our Father who is in heaven.

11
Metamorphosis

You could measure by the wiggles of Bubu's tail his contempt for tadpoles who couldn't think. His experience as chairman of the Little Pond Philosophical and Debating Society had impressed on him not only the importance of reason but also the penetrative ability of his own mind.

Of course, not everybody had Bubu's background. His years in Tadpole University had opened his eyes to a lot. There had been the free intellectual give-and-take of his undergraduate days. Later, working on the staff as lecturer and research assistant, Bubu saw his book *Tail Wiggle Coefficients as an Index to Social Maladjustment* published and felt he had opened a new era in understanding aquatic behavior characteristics. Largely unappreciated outside academic circles, the audacity of its revolutionary concepts had exploded powerfully among the intellectual elite. When the work was discussed, tempers flared and the friendships of years were broken. Yet the masterpiece failed to gain for Bubu the chair he had hoped. His had been the misfortune of developing ideas fifty years ahead of their time.

Yet hadn't the university's loss been society's gain? Hadn't the Philosophical and Debating Society, which he had founded, disseminated light among the inhabitants of Little Pond? The reflection comforted him as he wiggled gently among soft curtains of sunlight in the cool green waters.

Not all Little Ponders had shown appreciation. The mental horizons of most of them were bounded by the pond itself. If life existed in the streams that entered and left it, it was a strange, foreign life. And who was to know what lay beyond in the lakes and oceans of which scientists spoke? Vast distances, infinite spaces. Empty and hostile? Filled with other forms of life? What life could inhabit the salty vastness that scientists described? While such speculation sent delicious intellectual shivers to the tip of Bubu's tail, they left most Little Ponders cold. Patiently Bubu tried to teach them the value of intellectual speculation checked by careful experiment and cold reason.

Bubu became abruptly aware of someone at his side. Powerful thrusts from a frog's vigorous legs had propelled him next to Bubu. The frog was a new member of the Philosophical Society and Bubu greeted him warmly. Though the frog appeared to Bubu to be bound by superstition and subjectivism, he nevertheless showed promise.

"Beautiful day," said Bubu.

"Beautiful," agreed the frog. "And up above it's tremendous. I never knew such colors existed before my conversion."

If Bubu was embarrassed, he gave no sign of it. "I don't doubt your sincerity in the least," he murmured smilingly, "though from my reading in psychology I suspect that your conversion is merely a psychological phenomenon."

The frog looked puzzled. "Well, it's a phenomenon, anyway. I know I'm different from what I was before." He looked at Bubu's quivering tail and then at his own powerful muscles. "For instance, I can do things now that I never used to be able to do."

Bubu grew solemn. Had he possessed eyebrows and fingertips, he would have raised the former and placed the latter together. "You are different because you *think* you are different. I personally have observed the difference, and it confirms all I have come to believe about the overwhelming influence of mind over body. Indeed, I might amplify my statements. Conversion is more than a psychological phenomenon. It's a psychosomatic phenomenon."

The frog looked mischievous. "I'm not sure what psychosomatic phenomena are. But if my legs are an example, then I'm all for psychosomatic phenomena." And as if to underline his remark, he vigorously propelled himself in a swift circle before settling down beside Bubu once more.

But then he asked Bubu, "You mean that my legs are in some way unreal?"

Bubu was at home now. "Not at all. I'm not sure, of course, what you mean by *real*, but if you mean what I think you mean, I would say that your legs are the real result of your faith in something unreal. I noticed that you began to develop them about the same time you started talking about your fantastic 'world' of 'air' and 'sunlight' and 'insects.' I can only conclude that your belief in this unreal subjective experience of yours is responsible for the creation of your real legs."

The frog began to look interested. "You mean that unreality plus faith equals reality? That raises some interesting issues."

Bubu was not to be put off. "Exactly," he cried, swelling visibly. "Take hypnosis, for instance. If I were to hypnotize you and then tell you that you had been drinking heavily, you'd start behaving like a drunken frog."

"But that wouldn't be real drunkenness, and there would be no alcohol in me."

"No, but the change in you would be real. What's more, I could produce actual physical changes in you. I might, while you were still hypnotized, tell you that I was about to strike you a heavy, painful blow. I could then touch you lightly, and my touch would produce a real bruise. Your belief in an imaginary blow would have produced real harm."

"And my legs are like the bruise resulting from an imaginary blow?"

"Precisely."

The frog hated to say it, but he could see no alternative. "Then why, Bubu, don't you go to a hypnotist and get yourself a pair of legs? That would be better than a bruise and much more useful than your tail. I got rid of mine soon after my own legs began to function."

Bubu's swelling subsided. "It has to be admitted," he said, a shade too casually, "that there are at present limits to what hypnotists and psychologists can do. But that's because our techniques haven't advanced sufficiently. The principle of the thing remains. Once we've developed more powerful psychotherapy, we shall be able to produce the same miracles as you.

"Though for myself," he continued, "I prefer to be intellectually honest. I refuse to exploit the cheap benefits that come from living in a world of fantasy. I cannot sacrifice my integrity and believe in what I know to be untrue, even if by doing so I could gain a pair of legs. In any case, your exhibitionistic cavortings don't appeal to me." The tiny tadpole's dignity seemed pitiful as he quivered beside the frog's vigorous young body.

Something akin to pity filled the frog's eyes as he looked at him. "But Bubu," he said quietly, "the world up above that I talk about is real. I can't explain it, but in a sense it's more real than the watery universe we live in."

"More real *to you*."

"More real to anybody, Bubu."

"But not at all real to me."

The frog had lost his bantering manner entirely. "Bubu, the world would be there whether I could feel it or not. It's still there even though you don't believe in it. Right now, as we talk, soft breezes blow across the surface of Little Pond. A burning sun pours rays over the bodies of animals, birds and plants. Other frogs like me are leaping across dry ground."

"It is very beautiful," the tadpole said precisely, his tone belying his words, "but I don't even understand what you mean. What, for instance, is *dry*? No, don't try to describe it again." (The frog had been about to interrupt.) "You've failed to give me any but the most *mystical* concept whenever I've asked about it. Can dry be weighed? Does dry have length or depth? Can dry be touched? Does it have color? To all of this you answer no.

"As far as I can gather, dry seems merely to be the essence of 'otherness,' the opposite of all we've come to accept as being fundamental to the watery universe we know. I shall believe it when you can produce solid evidence."

The frog stretched out a webbed foot. "My legs, Bubu, aren't they evidence?"

The tadpole made a gesture of impatience, but the frog continued, "The universe we inhabit is evidence of the 'other world,' as you call it. Our world grows gray when clouds cover the sun. The surface of our pond is thrashed into a fury when rain dashes on it from the world above."

It was then that Bubu's eloquent tail wiggled its derisive contempt. "Ignorant people have always explained purely natural phenomena in terms of myth. Science has adequately explained these. There's no need to postulate a dry world populated by mysterious suns, moons, clouds."

"Bubu, I've seen clouds. I've been warmed by the sun. I—"

The tadpole's annoyance nearly choked him. "Show me!" he cried. "Show me this sun. Show me a piece of dry."

There was a pause, filled only with soft underwater sounds.

"I have to admit," the frog said finally, "that it's impossible for me to show you the sun. If you are to see it, your eyes will have to change. There's a verse in the Sacred Book that says, 'Except a tadpole metamorphose, it cannot see the kingdom of dryness.' I'd like you to see and know what I see and know. I hope one day to take you hopping with me between blades of grass. But if I took you right now, just as you are, you'd die. You couldn't stand the exposure. You don't have the right kind of life.

"A few moments ago you told me that my belief in these things had produced my legs and lungs. Maybe. But that's far from the whole story. It's just as true and far more important for you to see that without my lungs and legs I could never live on land. My conversion, or my metamorphosis, was a gateway into a new world. The more I saw of it, the more I changed; and the more I changed, the more I was able to see."

There was again no answer. The tadpole's tail was scarcely waving at all.

"The vital question," the frog continued, "is whether you're willing to follow the evidence where it leads. You'll not be given more evidence until you use the evidence you have."

Bubu said something that sounded like "Humph."

Again there was silence.

The frog stretched his legs uneasily. "It's so stuffy down here," he said, "I have to go up for a gulp of air more frequently these days. So if you'll excuse me . . ."

Underwater etiquette is not very rigid, and the frog darted away without finishing his sentence, thrusting powerfully upward through sunbeam curtains toward the surface of a world that did not exist.

Several minutes passed before Bubu moved. The wiggles of his tail had ceased. Slowly, with another "Humph," he emerged from the cover of a weed and moved in the direction that the frog had taken moments before.

Perhaps weighty problems occupying his mind accounted for the sluggishness of his movements. He might have been thinking of the brilliant remarks he could have made had he thought of them in time or gloating over the masterly way he would put the young frog in his place at the next meeting of the Philosophical Society.

His actual thoughts will never be known, for in his preoccupation he hadn't noticed the swiftly moving black shadow inches above him.

The duck's bill churned violently downward. Bubu was sucked by thrashing, whirling eddies. Immense jaws clamped on his tail, while his body tugged helplessly in the water. He felt himself jerked powerfully upward. Upward and, oh, unnamable dread, through the surface and into the Great Beyond.

Terrible light and suffocating nothingness surrounded him for a brief second. Sounds of unbelievable intensity battered his tortured hearing apparatus. Then, with a swift toss of the duck's head, came hot darkness.

12
Examining
the Evidence

_____Some people admire Christianity and would like to be able to believe it is true. They *would* believe if they *could*, but honestly they *can't*. Such people are divided between deep admiration of superb moral teaching and mild embarrassment over the "legends" surrounding the birth, death and alleged resurrection of the Teacher.

The tension can be resolved by being honest. Far from throwing away our intellectual integrity, we will need to guard it with extra care if we are to believe. Faith does not spring from pious ignorance but demands a willingness to accept the implications of evidence.

What implications of what evidence? The implications of the historical evidence relating to the birth, life, death and resurrection of the founder of Christianity. If he *is* God, then he has every right to impose his standards rigidly on our lives. He would have the right to decide how we should dispose of our income, whom we may marry, how we should live and when we will die. Our decision would be a loaded one. Today's friends could become tomorrow's critics. Therefore, feeling that it would be "nice" to "be able to" believe is as far from realistic as is any underlying assumption that it implies a regression to simple credulity.

The historical evidence is found in the Bible, and we need only encourage people to examine it openly and honestly. "Faith comes from what is heard, and what is heard comes by the preaching of Christ" (Rom 10:17). To talk about historical evidence in one breath and a "holy" book in the next seems nonsense. It is one matter to respect the Bible, but aren't we being naive to expect everyone else to feel the same way about it as we do?

Not at all. The Book which has become so sacred to many of us has become so, precisely because we have examined it honestly. We began (many of us) by treating it as what it is— a collection of early documents reporting and interpreting historical events. And, as the weight of evidence bore in, faith was born. Our initial approach was not likely always a religious one. In some cases it was frankly skeptical. But the evidence itself convinced us. Since the truths to which the evidence led were transcendental, we had little difficulty in later accepting the claim the documents made to be divinely inspired records.

Unfortunately, the same evidence has not convinced everybody. It has nearly always provoked some reaction— as often as not, a violent one. Just as the true preaching of the evidence has resulted in either riots or revivals, so the private examination of it has provoked both repentant faith and bitter hostility.

Yet sometimes a reaction of any kind is missing. Some can approach the Bible with built-in mental sets. As C. S. Lewis pointed out in *The Screwtape Letters,* such a person has "a dozen incompatible philosophies dancing about together in his head. He doesn't think of doctrines as primarily 'true' or 'false,' but as 'academic' or 'practical,' 'outworn' or 'contemporary,' 'conventional' or 'ruthless.' " He lives in a schizophrenialike museum, keeping ideas in glass cases, as specimens to be catalogued. The glass he uses must continually be reinforced since ideas, especially true ones, are hard to kill, threatening always to wreck his cowardly, academic peace by smashing their way to freedom.

Let us therefore invite our friends to examine the Bible, to throw away their prejudice and to abandon their defenses against fear. They need not make any decision in advance. We should ask them merely to have the courage to face certain writings honestly and to shun pseudointellectualism. There is no need to shut truth in glass cases. Truth is only dangerous when we try to control it and manipulate it.

For, as they will discover if they accept your challenge, truth is a Person—a Person who refuses to be controlled or manipulated. His portrait confronts us in first-century documents. He emerges from written pages to repeat to us his challenge to the original doubter, "Put your finger here, and see my hands; and . . . do not be faithless, but believing" (Jn 20:27).

13
Parable
of the
Orange Trees

_____ I dreamed I drove on a Florida road, still and straight and empty. On either side were groves of orange trees. As I turned to look at them from time to time, line after line of trees stretched back endlessly from the road, their boughs heavy with round yellow fruit. This was harvest time. My wonder grew as the miles slipped by. How could the harvest be gathered?

Suddenly I realized that for all the hours I had driven (and this was how I knew I must be dreaming), I had seen no other person. The groves were empty of people. No other car had passed me. No houses were to be seen beside the highway. I was alone in a forest of orange trees.

But at last I saw some orange pickers. Far from the highway, almost on the horizon, lost in the vast wilderness of unpicked fruit, I could discern a tiny group of them working steadily. And many miles later I saw another group. I could not be sure, but I suspected that the earth beneath me was shaking with silent laughter at the hopelessness of their task. Yet the pickers went on picking.

The sun had long passed its zenith, and the shadows were

lengthening when, without any warning, I turned a corner to see a notice, "Leaving NEGLECTED COUNTY— Entering HOME COUNTY." The contrast was so startling that I scarcely had time to take in the notice. I had to slow down, for all at once the traffic was heavy. People by the thousands swarmed the road and crowded the walks.

Even more startling was the transformation in the orange groves. Orange groves were still there, and orange trees in abundance. But now, far from being silent and empty, they were filled with the laughter and singing of multitudes of people. Indeed it was the people I noticed rather than the trees. People—and houses.

I parked the car at the roadside and mingled with the crowd. Smart dresses, classy shoes, expensive suits and starched shirts made me a little conscious of my work clothes. Everyone seemed so fresh and poised, so happy.

"Is it a holiday?" I asked a well-dressed woman with whom I fell in step.

She looked a little startled for a moment, and then her face relaxed with a smile of gracious condescension.

"You're a stranger, aren't you?" she said, and before I could reply, "This is Orange Day."

She must have seen a puzzled look on my face, for she went on, "It is so good to turn aside from one's labors and pick oranges one day of the week."

"But don't you pick oranges every day?" I asked her.

"One may pick oranges at any time," she said. "We should always be ready to pick oranges, but Orange Day is the day that we devote especially to picking."

I left her and made my way further into the trees. Most of the people were carrying a book. Bound beautifully in leather, edged and lettered in gold, the book bore on its spine the title "Orange Picker's Manual."

By and by I noticed that around one of the orange trees seats had been arranged, rising upward in tiers from the ground. They were almost full—but, as I approached the group, a smiling well-dressed gentleman shook my hand and conducted me to a seat.

There, around the foot of the orange tree, I could see a number of people. One of them was addressing all the people on the seats and, just as I got to my place, they all rose to their feet and began to sing. The man next to me shared his song book with me. It was called *Songs of the Orange Groves*.

They sang for some time, and the song leader waved his arms with a strange and frenzied abandon, exhorting the people in the intervals between the songs to sing louder.

I grew steadily more puzzled.

"When do we start to pick oranges?" I asked the man who had loaned me his book.

"It's not long now," he told me. "We like to get everyone warmed up first. Besides, we want to make the oranges feel at home." I thought he was joking—but his face was serious.

After a while a rather fat man took over from the song leader and, after reading two sentences from his well-thumbed copy of the Orange Picker's Manual, began to make a speech. I wasn't clear whether he was addressing the people or the oranges.

I glanced behind me and saw a number of groups of people similar to our own group gathering around an occasional tree and being addressed by other fat men. Some of the trees had no one around them.

"Which trees do we pick from?" I asked the man beside me. He did not seem to understand, so I pointed to the trees round about.

"This is our tree," he said, pointing to the one we were gathered around.

"But there are too many of us to pick from just one tree," I protested. "Why, there are more people than oranges!"

"But we don't pick oranges," the man explained. "We haven't been called. That's the Chief Orange Picker's job.

We're here to support him. Besides we haven't been to college. You need to know how an orange thinks before you can pick it successfully—orange psychology, you know. Most of these folk here," he went on, pointing to the congregation, "have never been to Manual School."

"Manual School," I whispered. "What's that?"

"It's where they go to study the Orange Picker's Manual," my informant went on. "It's very hard to understand. You need years of study before it makes sense."

"I see," I murmured. "I had no idea that picking oranges was so difficult."

The fat man at the front was still making his speech. His face was red, and he appeared to be indignant about something. So far as I could see there was rivalry with some of the other orange-picking groups. But a moment later a glow came on his face.

"But we are not forsaken," he said. "We have much to be thankful for. Last week, we saw *three oranges brought into our baskets,* and we are now completely debt-free from the money we owed on the new cushion covers that grace the seats you now sit on."

"Isn't it wonderful?" the man next to me murmured. I made no reply. I felt that something must be wrong somewhere. All this seemed a very roundabout way of picking oranges.

The fat man was reaching a climax in his speech. The atmosphere seemed tense. Then, with a dramatic gesture, he reached for two of the oranges, plucked them from the branch and placed them in the basket at his feet. The applause was deafening.

"Do we start picking now?" I asked my informant.

"What in the world do you think we're doing?" he hissed. "What do you suppose this tremendous effort has been made for? There's more orange-picking talent in this group than in the rest of Home County. Thousands of dollars have been spent on the tree you're looking at."

I apologized quickly. "I wasn't being critical," I said. "And I'm sure the chief must be a very good orange picker —but surely the rest of us could try. After all, there are so many oranges that need picking. We've all got a pair of hands, and we could read the Manual."

"When you've been in the business as long as I have, you'll realize that it's not as simple as that," he replied. "There isn't time, for one thing. We have our work to do, our families to care for, our homes to look after. We . . ."

But I wasn't listening. Light was beginning to break on me. Whatever these people were, they were not orange pickers. Orange picking was just a form of entertainment for their weekends.

I tried one or two other of the groups around the trees. Not all of them had such high academic standards for orange pickers. Some held classes on orange picking. I tried to tell them of the trees I had seen in Neglected County, but they seemed to have little interest.

"We haven't picked the oranges here yet," was their usual reply.

The sun was almost setting and, growing tired of the noise and activity all around me, I got in the car and began to drive back again along the road I had come. Soon all around me again were the vast and empty orange groves.

But there were changes. Something had happened in my absence. Everywhere the ground was littered with fallen fruit. And as I watched it, it seemed that before my eyes the trees began to rain oranges. Many of them lay rotting on the ground. It was all so strange, and my bewilderment grew as I thought of all the people in Home County.

Then, booming through the trees came a voice: "The harvest truly is plentiful, but the laborers are few; pray therefore the Lord of the harvest to send out laborers . . ."

Then I awakened.

14
Dos Comunistas

When I worked with Christians in the universities of Latin America, we did not try to beat Communism. We tried (among other things) to win Communists.

Communists are people. They live, hate, fear, rejoice, marry, beget children, have souls, die, are buried, and will one day face God in judgment. In these respects they are fellow human beings, created in God's image. So we sought to reach them. We did so because we were under God's orders to reach all students (and for that matter, all men and women) with the gospel.

In trying to reach Communist students, we sometimes got nowhere. We knew failure, but we also knew triumph. Consider, for example, the following two case histories.

Pepe: Failure, Pro Tem

When I first met Pepe (not his real name), he was attending the meetings of the student group sponsored by the International Fellowship of Evangelical Students in Panama. He was a young, Spanish-speaking Black who was a member of a Pentecostal church. He was the kind of student you liked on the spot—lean, eager, round-eyed, stuttery, with a shy crooked smile that won your heart. Everybody teased him, for he was just the kind of fellow you had to tease. And he took it well.

At a Christian student conference in Panama, he rose to my bait when I asked him publicly why he attended Communist student meetings. No, he wasn't a Communist, he cried as he leapt to his feet. But he did admire Communists. They really believed what they said. They did things. He implied that evangelical students didn't believe what they said and that they were tepid in comparison with their Communist colleagues. His comment caused quite a fuss.

I had thrown a puppy among the chickens, and the chickens fluttered and clucked.

When a trip was organized to see the Panama Canal locks, Pepe tried to needle the courteous official who showed us around. Why wasn't the Panama flag flying alone on the masthead of ships that came through the canal? (This was before the canal was turned over to Panama.) Were they not sailing through Panamanian territory? The official refused to get annoyed, but Pepe kept on needling. Some of the students told him to pipe down. They shared his feelings about the canal, but they were embarrassed by his blunt expression of them. After all, the Christian gringos were being decent. You just don't say things like Pepe was saying. He had no sense of propriety.

Three years later when I passed through Panama, I missed him. Where was Pepe? A friend, Les Archer, told me that he had stopped attending the group. He was around town somewhere, but he was lying low. He had disappeared altogether after some recent riots.

Had he joined the Party? Les couldn't say.

I visited Panama again on the day after General Mac-Arthur's death. Les Archer picked me up at the airport. As we drove through part of Panama City, my eyes took in the fluttering flags (stars and stripes at half-mast, Panamanian flag at the top of the mast), the smashed traffic lights, and the burnt-out shell of a Pan-American Airways building (*Pan-American* had been reduced by the flames to *Pan can*). I asked about the student group and gathered that, although they had their views about the recent riots, they evidently sensed that loyalty to Christ was the highest loyalty. Solicitously they had visited the American missionary who was adviser to the group, checking each day to make sure he and his family were well.

What of Pepe?

"He disappeared for a while right after the riots."

"You mean . . ."

"Yes, I guess he was in the forefront of the organization of it."

"Is he a Party member?"

"Evidently."

"Does he ever come near the group?"

"No, he keeps clear. He doesn't want to see us."

Some months before, Les told me, Pepe had been caught crossing the frontier into Panama. Government officials confiscated the stuff they had found.

"What stuff? Arms?"

"No, literature. Propaganda."

"From Cuba?"

"No, he'd been in Russia."

"I see." I thought of the bright-eyed kid and his half-shy smile. A revolutionary. A bundle of emotions in the hands of people who could put his emotions to good use.

"He and his father live in a nice apartment in a good part of town," Les continued. "They couldn't possibly earn enough money to pay for it. The money must come from abroad."

I said nothing. There was nothing to be said.

Pedro: You Just Never Know

Pedro's case was different.

René Padilla was worried. The student group in Quito, Ecuador, which he regularly visited in his travels, was feeble and apathetic. But one or two of the students seemed to show a faint glimmer of hope. At times the glimmer almost disappeared, but other times, perhaps in a camp or in a Saturday-afternoon Bible study, René and his brother Washington would be heartened by some sign that the Holy Spirit was still on the job.

There were only a handful of students. They used to meet in the sala of Washington Padilla's house, not far from the studios of radio station HCJB in Quito. René and Washington wanted to get the idea of inductive Bible study across to them.

At first it didn't go over too well. They showed the same sort of enthusiasm that you get when you try to start a discussion about metaphysical poetry on a Sunday-school picnic. But Washington was patient, and one or two of the students showed signs of beginning to grasp the point.

The big problem was Pedro.

Pedro (once again, not his real name) was uninterested in what the Bible said. He was interested in expressing his own ideas. He wore heavy, horn-rimmed glasses, was beginning to grow fat, and was just a little pompous. Moreover, his remarks had the Pied-Piper-of-Hamlin quality that led all the other students after him; if not enchanted, they were at least ready to do battle over some question Pedro had raised.

There was good reason for this. Pedro was a graduate. He taught at the university, and this added weight to what he said.

His views also touched on politics—a fascinating and important subject in Latin America. Until the glory of the invisible breaks through, Bible study has a job competing with politics, especially if you are dealing with the politics of the extreme left. And Pedro was way, way left. He was, in fact, a member of the Communist Party. He had been jailed for his political activities.

These facts were not what worried René primarily. Nor was René afraid the group might "go left." René's concern, and Washington's too, was that the political issue, which should have been secondary, was diverting attention from hearing what God had to say. Just when the Padillas had hoped the students were beginning to get the idea of Bible study and witness, the students were in danger of selling their birthright for a mess of pottage.

René wrote me a long letter about it.

Three years later, having forgotten all about Pedro, I landed in Quito and waited, shivering a little with the dampness and cold of the rainy season in the Andes. Washington came buzzing up to the airport entrance in a little Volkswagen, his face warm and happy with welcome. In no time I was driving home with him. We chatted as the VW dodged around the wide Quito buses.

Washington was enthusiastic about the profound change in the group since my last visit. The students now knew where they were going. The president of the group, on his own initiative, regularly went over to the student dormitory to hold discussions with his non-Christian friends.

Washington described some of the students to me.

"One of them used to be a Communist," he said.

"Oh?" I had forgotten about Pedro.

"Yes, he used to be an awful nuisance. René felt we should ask him to stop attending."

The wheels slowly began to turn in my mind.

Washington continued, "But you know, I couldn't ask him to stop coming. I just couldn't do it. I felt that we must be patient with him. You just never know . . ."

"What happened in the end?"

"Well, he kept on attending the Bible studies."

"Were they the means of his conversion?"

"Well, he wasn't converted during a Bible study, though it was really the Bible studies that led to the conversion. He says that himself. But he said that one Sunday he was passing a church during the evening service, and he felt that he ought to go inside. He didn't know why he felt that way; he just did, that's all. So he went in."

"And he was converted?"

"Apparently."

"Is there a change in him?"

"Very definitely, yes. I wouldn't call him a spiritual leader, but his whole outlook and attitude have changed."

"Is he still a Communist?"

"No, and the authorities seem to recognize this. When there was a purge of leftist teachers in the university recently, he wasn't even considered for dismissal."

I was impressed.

"The other week when I was away," Washington continued, "he gave a kind of testimony to the group. He said that when he thought of the *tonterías* ("idiotic things") he used to say in the group, he was amazed at the patience I had had with him."

I began to remember, as Washington talked on, how I had replied three years before to René's letter.

"I think you are quite right," I had written. "It would be wiser to ask him to quit coming to the group. Better get rid of one man than jeopardize the whole group."

As Washington put it—you just never know.

God the Holy Spirit is still sovereign. He is no respecter of persons and has no favorites among nations. He is grieved by a person's rebellion rather than by the politico-religious coloring (red, purple, blue) it may take on. In his sovereign mercy he is speaking in Latin American universities to Communists, to Catholics, to evangelicals. We want to collaborate with him by yielding our lips and our lives to him.

You too may collaborate by yielding to him, by kneeling down to pray.

Part III
Christian
Discipleship

15
Absolute
Lord

What happens when the old patterns of our lives are smashed and we are set free forever to be slaves of Jesus Christ?

For the apostle Paul there was a blinding light, a voice that spoke from heaven and choking dust in his nostrils. He knew what for years he had been trying not to know, that Jesus of Nazareth was supreme in the universe. For Thomas there came the moment of burning shame as he heard the quiet words "Put your fingers here . . ." All doubts about who Jesus was were forever set at rest.

Whether through terror or shame, both men were gripped by the impression that Jesus was more than a mere man. He was Lord of creation. Paul had denied it and Thomas had doubted it, yet both now confessed with their lips what their lives continued to confess thereafter, "Lord . . ."

"My Lord and my God!" The knowledge of who Christ really is may not come to us so dramatically. We may not be thrown to our faces or confronted with Christ's physical presence. Yet however the Holy Spirit does it, whether he

uses someone's preaching or our own reading and meditation, he must bring us to the point where we cry out with
Paul and Thomas, "My Lord and my God!" And we must
cry out not only from our hearts but from our minds. We
must understand *why* and *how* Jesus Christ is pre-eminent.

The Conquering Lord

Jesus Christ has the right to rule in every area of our lives
because he has conquered sin and death. In these realms
earthly governments are powerless. The best government
and the police can do is to try to keep evil in check, just as
individuals can try to control their own evil bent. But unless
we have help from the outside, we are powerless in the
hands of sin and death, our real masters. Where is the gov-
ernor or the individual who is not subject to sin and death?
Yet Jesus Christ has judged sin and death. He has been
declared the Son of God with power by rising from the dead
(Rom 1:4).

Jesus Christ has the right to rule in every area of our lives
because he has overcome our previous masters by humbling himself to a death of public ignominy. Many earthly
rulers pretend to humble themselves. Candidates for office
often boast of their working-class origin or see to it that the
press publishes pictures of them shaking hands with poor
people. Why? Because it is recognized that those who rule
must have first-hand experience of the problems of those
they rule over. Jesus qualifies.

No one has humbled himself so completely as Christ, who
hid his glory from our view. He came to earth and became
not only a human being but a member of a working-class
home. Christ knew hunger, criticism, weakness and loneli-
ness, and he ended up pilloried to a shameful gibbet as if a
common criminal. He became identified with the people he
came to govern. In return for his suffering, God "highly
exalted him and bestowed on him the name which is above

every name, that at the name of Jesus every knee should bow" (Phil 2:9-10).

But once having understood *why* Christ rules, we must see *how* he rules. In what sense is he supreme?

Lord of History, Lord of Truth

Jesus Christ is, first of all, the Lord of history, actively involved in the world's politics. He is cognizant of tomorrow's revolutions in Africa and Latin America. He has his hand on the stock exchange and in U.S. presidential elections. As Lord, Jesus Christ knows the name of the next Soviet premier and is supreme in every decision made.

The Scriptures declare that "God has put all things in subjection under his [God the Son's] feet" (1 Cor 15:27). What do "all things" include? All the things that God has controlled from the dawn of history. He has control over the affairs of earthly rulers. "The king's heart is a stream of water in the hand of the LORD; he turns it wherever he will" (Prov 21:1). Christ shares in this ruling supremacy.

Many find it difficult to believe that Jesus Christ is writing history. But running the world is not our job. It is his responsibility. And we may rest in the ability of his powerful hands, once pierced for our sins.

Jesus is not only Lord of history, but he is the Lord of all knowledge. He has the final answers to the deepest questions people have ever asked. Does life have meaning? Why are we here? Why do we suffer? Is there a God? What is he like?

Scientists cannot answer these questions because God cannot be analyzed in a test tube or under a microscope. His handiwork can be examined, but this will not give final answers. The greatest of philosophers have long realized what scientists are now discovering—if we rely only on our own minds and observations, we can never know if God exists, and if he exists, what he is like. "Can you find out the deep things of God?" asked Zophar (Job 11:7). The answer is clear. Not just by searching into what he has made.

But thank God we do not have to rely on our own powers of investigation. A voice has spoken from the silence. Christ entered history. If men and women let him, Christ can illumine their minds. No one can have true knowledge apart from him. He is "the true light that enlightens every man" (Jn 1:9).

Our relationship with Jesus determines the extent to which he will enlighten our minds. If our minds are to glow with understanding, they need to be quickened with life. They need to be controlled by the Lifegiver. We must allow him to control our logic and bring our thoughts into captivity to him (2 Cor 10:5). In doing so we "will know the truth, and the truth will make [us] free" (Jn 8:32).

Lord of the Church, Lord of the Little

Jesus is also Lord of the church. The church is not a democratic institution, for final authority is vested neither in its members nor in its officers, but in Jesus Christ. Christ requires of the church a deeper personal loyalty and dedication than any dictator. The church today does not need men and women with a defiant spirit, but people who dread displeasing the Head of the church. Is Christ the author of the pastor's sermons? Is he the wisdom of the church board, or does the board vote the way the rich donor wants? Who is Lord of the church? Jesus or Mammon?

Christ is Lord of the little things in our lives too. For the little things are more important than the big. He must be the sovereign in all our affairs. The one "who is faithful in a very little" (that is, in money matters) will be faithful about the greater affairs of God's kingdom (Lk 16:10-11).

The question we must ask is, Was he the Lord of our behavior at breakfast this morning? Was he the Lord of our lips when supper burned? Is he the Lord over the resentment we cherish against others? The answer must be, Yes, he is. Jesus Christ is Lord. If we disobey him in small things, we are rebels.

Someday thrones and dominions will fall at the feet of Jesus, but we are not to wait till then. We are to worship him now. We must make him absolute Lord of the next sixty seconds, and then of all the little things we do in the next five minutes. We must make a new way of life that starts at once. We must be worthy of our worthy Lord.

"Worthy is the Lamb who was slain, to receive power and wealth and wisdom and might and honor and glory and blessing" (Rev 5:12). Amen!

16
Steps
of Faith

An agonized father, whose faith Jesus had challenged, cried, "I believe; help my unbelief" (Mk 9:24). This man's difficulty was not unique. Many people without faith wistfully long for it, while those who have it wish for more. Yet faith is neither mystical nor hard to acquire. It is not, as many people suppose, for a privileged class of men and women—the "natural believers."

One difficulty is that we do not all share the same view of what faith is. To some people faith is a kind of self-hypnosis, the sort that enables Fiji Islanders to walk bare-foot across red-hot coals without harm. Others, perhaps half-consciously, feel that faith is believing that untrue things are true. The more improbable the thing they believe, the greater their "faith."

Such ideas are far from the kind of faith that Jesus sought to inspire. If faith means believing lies, we are better off without it. The world has enough self-deception and es-capism already. And whether such "faith" parades in the guise of religion or under any other cloak, it shouldn't be called faith at all. It is only wishful thinking, and the fact that it may be *religious* wishful thinking makes it none the less despicable.

"Faith, fanatic Faith, once wedded fast to some dear falsehood, hugs it to the last," wrote Thomas More. A biting observation, but true. Nevertheless, real faith exists and its benefits are many.

Faith is a source of health. Most experienced doctors, whatever their religious views, admit its mysterious influence over the course of disease in some of their patients. Faith also produces emotional calm. Christians in all ages, their lives and faces bearing witness to their claims, have talked of inward peace under trying circumstances. As he ushered them into an epoch of pressure which was to mean imprisonment, terrible opposition and for some of them death, Jesus said to his disciples, "Peace I leave with you" (Jn 14:27). It was their faith that turned his words into reality.

Faith has enabled reformers to persist against impossible odds to ultimate triumph. It has given courage in battle, hope in despair, and calm in the face of danger and death. It enables us to recognize the power of ideals and truth, even though those who championed them died long ago.

But faith is more than these things. Its highest value lies in its use as a tool by which we may know things otherwise unknowable. Indeed its more immediate benefits spring from this. Faith, by biblical definition, is "the conviction of things not seen" (Heb 11:1). It is intangible and invisible, serving as a kind of gateway to a realm where other methods of arriving at knowledge will not help us.

Of course, we also use faith in the most matter-of-fact ways. Every time we sit on a chair, take a dose of medicine or eat a meal, we are acting by faith. We sit down, confident that the chair will support our weight. We take the medicine, believing that it will help us. We eat assuming the food is not poisoned.

Faith and Science

But faith comes into its true glory when it operates not within our space-time system but as a doorway leading us beyond it. By faith we can know (curious paradox) that God exists. By faith we can make his acquaintance. Only as we exercise faith will we be able to please him.

There are those who cavil at this time in the name of science. Such people speak not as scientists but as materialists when they say, "What I cannot prove I will not accept." Translated, this means, "The scientific method is a wonderful tool for discovering knowledge. What I cannot discover with this tool cannot be discovered. No other tool is any good."

Proof, of course, means different things to different people. (Most people use the word *scientific* rather loosely.) It would be defined one way by police officers, another way by lawyers and still another way by scientists. The end of knowledge to be established by each "proof" is of a different order. In one case we are dealing with human hate, fear, greed and guilt; in the other, the qualities of matter and energy. Naturally the proofs will differ.

This is important for it suggests that no such thing as absolute proof may exist. Proof is something arbitrary, a certain sum of evidence we demand before we accept something as fact. The amount and quality of evidence demanded will vary with who demands it and what she or he is concerned with. My proof might never satisfy you. What you regard as proof might make your lawyer smile. All of us have standards about how much evidence we require. But we do demand evidence.

Once this is grasped it becomes easy to see that the whole idea of proof, useful as it may be at times, should not make slaves of us. We should always demand evidence, but the kind of evidence will vary with the circumstances.

Thus faith need never be "blind" to be faith. Blind faith

says yes when the evidence says no. Christian faith says yes because the most important evidences say yes too. (The evidence does not meet all the requirements of "scientific proof." But we are not dealing with science. We are dealing with a realm in which science is helpless.)

Such evidence abounds. It is in our bodies and minds, in the natural order around us. It is found in historical documents that describe the words and actions of the man Jesus and of the prophets who preceded him. It is to be seen in the dead walls of the forgotten cities dug up by archaeologists, and in the glowing lives of transformed, modern sinners. Its volume is tremendous and its quality unparalleled.

How much documentary evidence is required before we believe something? Schoolchildren are confidently taught that Julius Caesar invaded Britain in 55 B.C. It occurs to no one to doubt it. Yet the earliest written evidence is in a ninth-century manuscript. Documentary evidence for the resurrection of Christ includes hundreds of early manuscripts, some going back to the second century. No other fact of ancient times is so fully attested.

Then where does faith come in? If the evidence for the truth of Christianity is so great, why do we need faith at all?

The evidence, it is true, is great. But for some of us it will still not be enough. Gaps exist. But faith, as Oliver Wendell Holmes once remarked, "is the acceptance of a greater fact and the rejection of a lesser." When you make up your mind that the weight of evidence points to the truth, you exercise faith. To reserve your opinion is to doubt. To decide against the evidence is to disbelieve.

Getting in the Wheelbarrow

Acknowledging the strength of the evidence is only the beginning of faith, however. In order to believe (in the Christian sense), you do not merely assent to certain propositions. You gamble your life on those propositions. You believe that God exists? Very well, bow down at his feet. You believe he is good? Then trust him enough to do whatever he tells you. You believe he can cure the ills of your soul? Then go to him for help.

Blondin, the great acrobat, in his bid for world acclaim had a tightrope stretched across Niagara Falls. Spellbound crowds watched him cross it, turn somersaults on it, push a wheelbarrow above the awesome plunging. The incredulity of New York newspapers turned to wondering admiration as eyewitness accounts multiplied. Blondin continued. His star was rising. Confidence in his prowess was growing.

"Do you believe I could push you across safely?" he asked one visiting celebrity.

"I do indeed" was the hearty reply.

"Then get in," said Blondin.

The celebrity declined.

Yet this is what faith is. Christian faith is to gamble your existence on the reliability of God, to "get in the wheelbarrow." Faith is to believe not only that God is but also that he rewards those who diligently seek him (Heb 11:7).

This is the kind of faith that turns people into Christians, and Christians into a power for good. Christians are not just church members or assenters to dogma. They are changed beings who enjoy through faith the forgiveness of their sins, and through whose bodies new life has begun to pulsate. They live. The Spirit of God has entered. They know what God is like for they know God.

Where does such faith come from? How can you find it?

Those who are not Christians of the kind I mentioned can, as I encouraged in chapter twelve, examine the evidence. Faith can be found in solid facts. So studying the biblical documents themselves is fundamental. The Gospel of John is a deliberate attempt to present non-Christian readers with the most important evidence. "These [things] are written," John says at the end of the book, "that you may believe that Jesus is the Christ, the Son of God, and that believing you may have life in his name" (Jn 20:31).

Studying with the right attitude, without prejudice and pride, is key. To study with an open mind one must study with a humble mind. Then one is able to understand the truth. We get nowhere if we study to prove our own theories. St. John was careful to record the words of Jesus: "If any man's will is to do his [God's] will, he shall know whether the teaching is from God or whether I am speaking on my own authority" (Jn 7:17).

My counsel for Christians who seek more faith is the same: go over the evidence, one more time. You will find it as firm as ever. Read the promises of Scripture too. Remember, "faith comes from . . . the word of Christ" (Rom 10:17 NIV).

In an old edition of Bunyan's *Pilgrim's Progress* Christian and his comrade are imprisoned in Doubting Castle. Giant Despair has seized the two pilgrims and has flung them into the dungeons below the castle. In the darkness, and after many days of cruel beatings, their spirits are low—until suddenly Christian remembers the key in his bosom. It is a golden key and its name is Promises. Eagerly thrusting it into the lock of their cell, they watch as the door swings open. One by one the creaking doors of Doubting Castle give way before Promises, until the pilgrims feel their backs warmed by the sun and their eyes dazzled by it.

Your faith will not grow as you look at it. Feed it. Give it the strong meat of the truth of God.

Trusting the Chief

Just as faith is not merely accepting facts but trusting a Person, so its final growth will only come as we get to know that Person. If our faith has introduced us to God in Christ, we should get to know him better. The more we know a trustworthy person, the greater our confidence in him becomes. Someone might tell us that God is trustworthy, but that is not enough. We need to find out for ourselves. We need to know him.

I was nervous. My wife was to have an operation. As I tried to think of whom I could trust to do the surgery, my misgivings multiplied until I remembered "the Chief." The Chief was my old professor of surgery whom I had known for years. I had seen him operate often. I had assisted him. For hours I had watched his deft, gloved hands confidently restore order in diseased human bodies. No crisis seemed to ruffle him; no problem baffled him.

As I thought about the Chief, my anxiety subsided. I could trust him because I knew him so well.

Do I doubt God's power? Or his concern for me? If so, I don't fully know him. Knowing him, I could never doubt his power or care. It is not more faith that I need to pray for —faith as a grain of mustard seed is enough—but to know God better.

It is time to abandon the idea that faith is a kind of leap into the dark. A leap it may be; or better, a step—followed by many more steps that become a walk and way of life. We might hesitate to take them, uncertain at first of the firmness of the ground ahead. That is what makes them steps of *faith*.

But they are not steps into the dark. As we take them, we find for ourselves that they are steps into light, which grows more and more into a perfect day.

17
God's
Perfect
Peace

_____As a medical doctor I have watched many patients being put to sleep under anesthetic. The frowns slip from their faces, and they seem to relax. But they don't have peace; they're just unconscious.

I have known people to die, defying God and blaspheming. Afterward their relatives have said, "Ah, now they have peace." But death is not peace either.

Nor do people find peace by calming their nerves or forgetting their worries. You can take tranquilizers to calm your nerves. You can watch television or fall asleep or practice transcendental meditation, and forget worry. But none of these gives peace.

Peace is a deep, heart experience that belongs by right to every Christian. "My peace I give to you," Jesus told the wondering disciples. "Not as the world gives do I give to you. Let not your hearts be troubled, neither let them be afraid" (Jn 14:27).

A Lighthouse in a Storm
Was he saying there would be no storms? Far from it. He was about to leave them and was sending them to face prob-

lems, opposition, imprisonment and violent death. But in the midst of hatred and persecution they were to have a supernatural gift—the peace of God. It would steady them in the face of threats; it would make them buoyant under a deluge of problems, carefree in poverty and sickness.

The heart that has this kind of peace is like a lighthouse in a storm. Winds shriek, waves crash, and lightning flickers around it. But inside, the children play while their parents go about their work. They may look out the window to marvel at the powers that rage around them, but they have peace—the peace of knowing that the strength that protects them is stronger than the strength of the storm.

This is "the peace . . . which passes all understanding" (Phil 4:7). It is peace "not as the world gives" (Jn 14:27). It is described by Isaiah as "perfect peace" and by the psalmist as "great peace." Isaiah also calls it "peace . . . like a river" (48:18)—that flows on and on. Exaggerated? Not a bit! When God does something, he does it properly.

What effects will peace of this kind have in your life? It will affect your body and mind. You may digest your food better and feel healthier. You may even sleep better (Ps 4:8). But far more important, this peace will have spiritual effects.

Peace is not just a psychological state; it is a spiritual gift. As such, it will have spiritual results. For instance, it will help you to be holy. In fact, you cannot live a holy life unless you first have peace. Peace, you see, doesn't exactly depend on victory; it paves the way for victory. If you lose your peace, you will also lose your victory!

Peace is also one of the fruits of the Spirit. If you lack peace, it is because something is hindering the work of the Holy Spirit in your life. This is what Paul means when he says, "Let the peace of Christ rule in your hearts" (Col 3:15). Peace is a kind of signal. Any lack of it is an alarm telling you that things have gone wrong.

How does the Holy Spirit give peace? He does so simply by convincing my heart about certain truths. When I sin, he seeks to convict me and to remind me of the cleansing blood. When doubts or fears rob me of peace, he seeks to turn me to the Word of God or to reassure me of God's great love for me.

This is important. We don't enjoy peace simply by *having* the Holy Spirit the way we take a drug. All we have to do is swallow a drug and it goes to work—calming us down or pepping us up. But the Holy Spirit is a Person, not a pill. He gives us peace when we let him open our eyes, when we collaborate with him.

Peace before Holiness
How do we collaborate with the Holy Spirit?

First, *by reading the Word of God.* An eminent psychiatrist once told a friend of mine that he recommended solid Bible study to all his neurotic patients. He was not a Christian, yet he had discovered the peace-giving effects of the Bible. "Great peace have those who love thy law," says the psalmist; "nothing can make them stumble" (Ps 119:165). In modern English the last part of the verse would read, "And nothing shall upset them."

Mind you, I am not saying that the Bible is a tranquilizer. Peace comes when the truth of the Bible throws light on our heart's problems. It becomes even deeper when we put what the Bible says into practice. "O that you had hearkened to my commandments!" cried God on one occasion. "Then your peace would have been like a river" (Is 48:18).

Is there something God has spoken to you about from his Word? Does he want you to do something but you are putting him off? Could this be the way you lost your peace? Well, it is not worth it. Give in to the Lord and do it. You will be amazed at the peace that will quietly fill your soul.

Second, we collaborate by letting the Holy Spirit teach us,

as we read the Bible, *the value of the blood of Christ*. Basically our peace comes "by the blood of his cross" (Col 1:20), that is, through the death of Christ which atones for our sins. Peace of heart is based on peace with God. Now, while in theory I know all about the blood, in practice I need to be reminded again and again that the death of God's Son satisfies him completely so far as I am concerned. I don't have to struggle to keep my peace with God. It is Christ's finished work that does this, not my struggles to live a victorious life.

I mention this because it's so easy to mistakenly feel that God will love us more if we achieve a more spiritual kind of life. He won't. He loves us for Christ's sake, not for our achievements' sake. Indeed, holiness itself is not an achievement. It's a gift of God's love. And it begins with peace. "Properly speaking, . . ." wrote Horatius Bonar, "the peace goes before the holiness and is its parent."[1]

Looking at the Blackboard

Third, we collaborate by getting into the habit of *fixing our eyes by faith on the Lord*. The psalmist spoke of the person whose "heart is firm, trusting in the LORD" (Ps 112:7). That's what we might call the firm look of faith. And Scripture guarantees it will result in peace. "Thou dost keep him in perfect peace," says Isaiah, "whose mind is stayed on thee, because he trusts in thee" (Is 26:3). So don't look at problems. Look at the Lord—fixedly.

This, too is important. If we have fears or anxieties that rob us of peace, the Holy Spirit will give us peace by making real to us the power and love of God. But we've got to cooperate. He can't make God's love and power real if we persist in fixing our minds on our problems. A teacher can only make the lesson plain to the pupils who are looking at the blackboard. The Holy Spirit is a teacher. Let us fix our gaze therefore on the One he wants to teach us about.

Finally, we gain peace *by being spiritually minded*. By this I mean looking at life from the Holy Spirit's point of view. Treasure in heaven is more important than security on earth. We should set our affections therefore on things above. In that way we won't be reduced to a nervous wreck when the stock market collapses or when our parents talk about divorce. For "to set the mind on the Spirit is life and peace" (Rom 8:6).

Some years ago on a seven-hour flight I settled down to pray. But, try as I might, I couldn't. I felt ill at ease and had no peace. I knew what the trouble was. It seemed likely that we'd have to move to another mission field where costs were high. After four years in Bolivia we had built an adobe house and had scraped some bits and pieces of furniture together. We could only sell at a loss. How could we manage in Argentina? Oh, I knew the Lord wouldn't let us starve, but I was unhappy.

Quietly I thought of a verse of Scripture, "I will never fail you nor forsake you." But it didn't work! It gave me no peace. Determined that it should, I opened my Bible and hunted it up. This is what I read: "Keep your life free from love of money, and be content with what you have; for he has said, 'I will never fail you . . .' " (Heb 13:5). I knew what was wrong at once. I was bothered about security on earth when I should have been thinking of treasure in heaven. I confessed my sin and my peace was restored.

Are you haunted by unrest? When carolers sing about "peace on earth," does it seem to you a mockery? Well, God is offering you a special gift. He paid a tremendous price for it, but he wants you to have it.

Give more time to his Word. Stop resisting God when he speaks to you through it. Ask him to teach you more about the blood of his Son. Stay your heart upon Jehovah. Stop fretting about earthly security. Seek treasure in heaven.

As you do so, you'll find a great, perfect, inconceivable, unearthly peace that flows on and on like a river.

18
Why
Quiet
Time?

_____I agree that quiet times work.

Regular sessions of prayer and Bible study produce changes—changes in us and changes in people around us.

I agree that our values alter once we start meeting regularly with God. Some things that once seemed important shrivel and lose their fascination, while others swell in significance. Seeing life through different eyes, we begin to adopt a heavenly perspective, growing more akin in our thinking to the celestial than to the earthly host. Inevitably we will influence people wherever we go, because we carry with us the smell of heaven. We will nauseate some and awaken in others a longing for Christ.

I agree that we will see people differently. We will pity people we once feared; eschew people we once cultivated; pray for people who once enraged us. The changes do not result because we mechanically follow rules, but because we have our new way of seeing, a new way of savoring life on earth.

We will, to be sure, approach problems differently, feel different about our work, our studies, our job, our future. Our goals will have changed so that life slowly takes on new meaning. The changes are understandable since we are influenced by the people we associate with. The more powerful or the more distinctive the characters of people we rub shoulders with, and the more time we spend with them, the greater the likelihood of change. It follows that if we spend time daily in the company of our Creator God, a profound impact will be made on our existence.

The changes need not be permanent. A tree that bends in the wind can straighten when the wind stops blowing. Leaves that turn from the shade will turn again when the shade is removed. But let the wind blow from the same quarter year in and year out to affect the tree's growth and development, and we shall observe a permanent molding in its shape. Or let the sun for years shine splendidly from above and we shall see great boughs spread symmetrically to rise sunward, and retain their form come darkness, earthquake, gale and blizzard.

So it is with time spent with God. A Christian, like a tree, never ceases to grow. As godly influences are incorporated, so changes which at first were temporary themselves become settled parts of our character that resist change. I agree, then, that to have a quiet time regularly will produce permanent and beneficial changes.

Peddling a Secret?

But do I recommend that we adopt the habit of a daily quiet time for these reasons? As a matter of fact, no. The changes are profound, but I don't want merely to peddle a secret in character development.

For one thing you may feel your character does not need to be changed. You may be satisfied with it as it is. And since I know nothing about you how can I discuss the matter? More important, Christians are not followers of Narcissus, the beautiful youth who gazed lovingly at his reflection in the water, but of Jesus. Narcissus' self-love led to drowning

—a fate which (psychologically) overtakes many of us in this age of self-cultivation. We may not exactly love ourselves, but we are forever gazing at our own psyches, primping and painting them in a fever of anxiety to satisfy our yearning for self-improvement. We yearn, not to admire another's beauty, but to become more beautiful ourselves.

My dilemma arises from the fact that while the practice of private devotions will indeed make you beautiful, the pursuit of personal loveliness is self-defeating. Paradoxically it is only as we forget our beauty or our lack of it and become lost in the enjoyment of the greatest beauty of all, that the changes I describe take place.

On what grounds then do I recommend the practice of private devotions? I could recommend it on many grounds. For instance, we lead limited lives. The earth has shrunk in the last fifty years. There are, I agree, mountains still to climb and submarine depths to explore. We could spend all our days investigating "spaceship earth" and its peoples and still have much to learn. But if size is anything to go by, then we are limited indeed. We live on the head of a pin for five minutes. Lost in vast reaches of space and time, lost by very reason of our smallness and our circumscription, our lives resemble popping flashbulbs seen from ten miles away.

Consider for a moment how you are trapped in time. We journey at a rate we have no control over. We cannot return to the past, our own or anyone else's, except in memory or imagination. Nor can we hurry ahead to see how the land lies and make provision for it. Controlled by powers we do not understand, we are driven by another in the prison-coach of time.

To commune with God on the other hand is to touch both infinity and eternity, not metaphorically but in very deed. We have opened a window to both a beyondness and an immediacy which time and space are powerless to provide and which we can experience in no other way. To that degree we have broken away from time-space to discover infinity close at hand. No astronaut can slip from beneath "the bonds of earth" more truly than he or she who touches God. Do you want to escape the confinement of a bodily existence? Meet God in your quiet time. He dwells in eternity and his being is infinite.

We are limited too in our contact with ideas and truth. The most widely read person among us has only rubbed shoulders with a few obscurity-bound professors or dipped into a selection of "the world's great books"—a contradictory jumble of finite perspectives. Yet we are invited to private tutorials with the fountain of ultimate wisdom; to a daily audience with the author of history; to fellowship and communion with the source of all holiness and love. There is no charge for such privileges. Yet strangely, we pour out our substance to purchase vastly inferior ones, scrabbling among straws and garbage while a jeweled crown is offered to us.

We are insane. The glories of heaven are ours for the taking. The wisdom of the ages is proffered free. We are bidden to bring our empty hearts to have them filled from cataracts of healing and love. Yet we remain earthbound, fuss enslaved, parochial minded and spiritually impoverished. We say we value heavenly things more than earthly, but our behavior contradicts our profession.

Of what value is the life you lead? What will your contribution amount to when the last and final examining board scrutinizes it? Will you have changed the course of history? And if so, for better, or for worse? Is there *any* value in your existence? Or are you destined to be a harmless cork, tossed about lightly on those streams of religious and secular culture that sweep us all from womb to tomb? You were enthused by a conference you attended. But for how long? What was its net effect on your usefulness? You were moved by a book you read. What permanent changes did it produce on your character or on the life you will lead ten years from now?

Yet we are invited to collaborate in the creation of destiny, not to be a mere spectator but a coauthor. God does not want to determine all things in splendid solitude by the word of his power. He wants the painting of the future to be a family project in which we all play a part under his benign direction. Earth's policy makers are but actors in a drama written in heaven, and we are offered a pen to do some of the writing. Can we imagine anything better?

I do not say that he intends to reveal to us in a few sessions the whole sweep of human destiny. To do so would pander to our vanity and create the illusion of knowing something that lies beyond our finite grasp. It is not for us to know the times and the seasons. Yet a child who is unable to appreciate the architectural know-how behind the design of a house or even to read blueprints, may still color the sketches of it, or help to build by knocking nails in boards. And both activities (coloring and hammering) are more satisfying to the child than comprehending the technicalities of the plan. Equally important, a *good* father is delighted to see his child joining in the work. We are called on to color and to build, not to become pseudoexperts on eschatology (Acts 1:1-8).

For Love's Sake

What reasons then can I give for the value of meeting regularly with God? Certainly we will escape the pettiness of the earthbound and commune with ultimate wisdom, infinity and love. Yet not even for these reasons, but for love's sake, would I urge us to meet God daily!

> As a hart longs
>   for flowing streams,
> so longs my soul
>   for thee, O God.
> My soul thirsts for God,

for the living God.
When shall I come and behold
the face of God? (Ps 42:1-2)

For love's sake we must seek him. For what he is, not for any
advantage we may gain. Our quest must be the quest of a
suitor, a suitor too blinded by beauty to descend to calculat-
ing self-interest; too intoxicated with love to care about the
cost or the consequences of his suit.

It must be the love of Mary, sitting at Jesus' feet, enchanted by his words and grace, but deaf and blind to the
frustration and fuss of her resentful sister (Lk 10:38-42).
An enchantment of that sort will not be broken, nor its
pleasures denied.

One thing have I asked of the LORD,
that will I seek after;
that I may dwell in the house of the LORD
all the days of my life,
to behold the beauty of the LORD,
and to inquire in his temple. (Ps 27:4)

It is time we threw spiritual pragmatism out of the window.
We come habitually to God carrying shopping baskets and
armed with a checklist of needed purchases when all the
time he wants to put his arms round us and draw us to himself. We know no other way. Custom and tradition have
drilled us in the art of celestial bargain hunting. It is time
we forgot about our spiritual performance and our spiritual needs and gave ourselves up to passion.

"Beautiful!" you sigh. "I wish I felt that way. But I don't
love God like that. So what can I do? How can I love when
my heart is cold, when all I experience is the nagging guilt
of knowing my love is a sorry thing not worth offering? Isn't
it hypocritical to force love? To go through the motions of
an unreal love?"

But wait. A moment ago when you read the words of the
psalmist, wasn't there a faint stirring of envy in you, an echo

of the longing the psalmist expressed? If there was—and it matters not how feeble or faint—then your love is not absent but suppressed. It lies dormant beneath the weight of unbelief and discouragement.

Unrequited love is painful. Rather than be tortured we bury our love where it will not disturb us by its insatiable demands. We *do* love. We long for that for which we were created and redeemed; but we suppress our longings, turn away from them, dam them up, silence them, lest their pain be insupportable.

Love is a hunger, and hunger can be suppressed. If you were to ask me during the hours and days when I keep my appetite at bay so I can devote myself to other compelling matters, "Aren't you hungry?" I would answer, "No, I don't think so. No—not in the least."

Yet place me in a chair, serve me a good meal and sit down to eat with me. Out of politeness I will arrange my napkin and begin to stick my fork in a piece of meat. And once the smell and the taste of the food assail my senses I will say, "My, that tastes good! Know what? I am hungry!"

So it is with love for God. It lies within many of us like a coiled spring, inactive but straining for release. It is a potential volcano, a dangerous thing that we fear to set free lest in failing to assuage it we shall have to cope with raging fire.

How we fear passion! Yet how great is our need to warm the cold mechanics of our daily routine at her fires! And who can guarantee that released longings will not lead to pain? I cannot.

Deep calls to deep
   at the thunder of thy cataracts;
All thy waves and thy billows
   have gone over me. . . .

I say to God, my rock:

"Why hast thou forgotten me?
Why go I mourning
    because of the oppression of the enemy?"

As with a deadly wound in my body,
    my adversaries taunt me,
while they say to me continually,
    "Where is your God?" (Ps 42:7, 9-10)

Our problem is not a want of yearning but a fear of releasing yearning from the grave where we have buried it. But unless we take the risk of loving, we will only be half alive. We belong among the living, not among the dead. Do not be afraid of the longing within; it is more than matched by the greater longing of a God who planted it there. He waits for our response and is not satisfied with our feeble prayer talk. He wants to know us intimately and to disclose to us the secrets of his heart.

Come, then, for love's sake. Come boldly defying fears. Enter into a love-pact to meet Christ daily. Come trembling to confess inadequacies. He is gentle and will understand. He will not force us or hurry the pace beyond what we are able to tolerate.

Come to his footstool. Come trusting. And come for love of him.

19
The Gift
of Guidance

What is God's will for my life? Should I marry? What church should I attend? What kind of work should I pursue? What school should I send my children to?

We all want to know what God wants for us. But how can we know for sure how he is guiding? These are all questions we ask ourselves frequently. And they are important questions. In addressing them, I would like to take up five areas: the personalness of guidance, the promise of guidance, the problems of guidance, the prerequisites of guidance and God's priorities in guidance.

The Heart of Guidance

Let me begin with the personalness of guidance.

Guidance is not mechanical. Some people predict a time when all automobile traffic will be guided by computers. You will be able to get into your car, press a button, and somebody somewhere or something somewhere will guide you to work. You won't have to do anything. Your car will not get too near to the car ahead, and the car behind will not get too near to you. You won't even have to worry about whether you're going along the right street because the computer will direct you along an alternate route if traffic is too heavy on the one that you would normally use.

I don't know whether that will ever happen, though some planners and dreamers say it will. But such guidance isn't personal, and there is no comfort to be drawn from it. Oh, I suppose you can feel sort of safe, but it's not the feeling you get when your neighbor says, "Come, I'll show you where the store is." If you are a new student on campus, bewildered by the new environment and strange procedures, what a relief to hear someone say, "I'll show you where the university bookstore is, and then I'll show you where you register"! The personal contact brings enormous comfort.

The heart and core of the guidance God gives is bound up in the personal relationship he wants to have with us. We don't have to look in the morning newspaper for the horoscope and try to figure out who the dark stranger is. Apart from being superstitious, it is impersonal. God's guidance is "him and me." He wants to guide me. He is interested in me. Not a sparrow falls to the ground without his knowing it. He knows all about me and all about my problems, all about my sins and all about the mess I've made. And he still wants to guide me. Herein lies the preciousness of guidance.

In Psalm 32:9 we read, "Be not like a horse or a mule, without understanding, which must be curbed with bit and bridle." Today the psalmist might say, "Be not like an automated car controlled by a computer that can't think for itself, that must be directed by a program." Instead, the Lord says, "I will counsel you with my eye upon you" (Ps 32:8). He watches and instructs and guides us individually.

God's guidance of the nation of Israel during their time in the wilderness was like this. They had many perplexing problems about when to fight and when not to fight, where to get food, where to find water and where to find pasture for their flocks. They were not short of worries. And we read Isaiah 63:9, "In all their affliction he was afflicted, and the angel of his presence saved them." It wasn't just a matter of the pillar of cloud and fire automatically doing their job. He was in their midst. And not only this, but in all their afflictions he was afflicted. He hurt with them—not from afar, not untouched in his regal splendor, but in their midst. This is guidance.

God walks beside us and wants to hold our hands in the perplexities of life. Jesus said, "My sheep hear my voice, and I know them, and they follow me" (Jn 10:27). Guidance is a highly personalized service. So many companies, especially those which provide mass-produced goods, like hamburgers, use commercials that try to make it seem as though there's a lot of personal care in what they offer. But everything they sell is the same to everyone who buys it. Not so with God's guidance. His interest in you as a person, his love for you, his concern for you, his desire that you be protected and led, is absolutely unique. To be guided by God is precious, not just because he gives the right directions, but because he gives fellowship with himself.

Generously to All

God has promised to continue to offer us his fellowship and guidance even when we turn away from him. "When my soul was embittered, when I was pricked in heart, I was stupid and ignorant, I was like a beast toward thee. Nevertheless I am continually with thee; thou dost hold my right hand. Thou dost guide me with thy counsel, and afterward thou wilt receive me to glory" (Ps 73:21-24). Even when we're stupid, ignorant and belligerent, he is still with us and we are still with him. And he will guide us with his counsel. This is his promise.

Let me turn then from the personalness of guidance to

the promise of guidance. Does God in fact promise it to us? Or was it just to David on a certain occasion that he promised it? Let me repeat one promise I've already quoted: "I will instruct you and teach you the way you should go" (Ps 32:8). And Isaiah 58:11 says, "The LORD will guide you continually." Ah, but you say, these might have been promises to Israel, to Isaiah, but not to me personally. I live in the twentieth century. Are there any promises *to me?*

Jesus, speaking to all his followers, says, "I will pray the Father, and he will give you another Counselor, to be with you for ever" (Jn 14:16). This is for all Christians. And the word is *Counselor,* the One who guides and directs. Elsewhere James writes, "If any of you lacks wisdom, let him ask God, who gives to all men generously and without reproaching" (Jas 1:5). To all men. It doesn't mean just all males. It means to everybody, to everybody who asks. We have to want it.

After we ask, how does he give? There are not a lot of conditions. There are no forms to fill in requiring details about your mother and father and where you were born and whether you're a citizen, whether you've ever been on welfare or whether you've got a criminal record. He knows all these things before he even offers you guidance. He doesn't rebuke us either. He doesn't say, "Oh, don't bother me now. I have the matters of the universe to look after. I have a new galaxy that I'm getting into place and it's rather tricky. Please don't come to me asking for guidance about something in the kitchen sink." He gives to all "generously and without reproaching." How certain is this promise? I haven't quoted the end of James 1:5 yet: "And it *will* be given him." It is certain. It's a promise.

The Problems of Guidance
It's all very well to say that God has promised to guide me, but exactly how does this happen? Do I have a vision? Do

words appear in letters of gold on the wall? This is the issue in our problems with guidance.

In the Old and New Testaments we read about people having dreams. Even today some people talk about being guided by God in dreams. I have no objection to being guided by dreams. The only caution I would add is that we should not regard dreams as a superior, or even a major form of guidance. Even when we do get a dream, we have to understand what the dream means. As a psychiatrist I know how puzzling that can be!

Are there other forms of guidance besides dreams? Certainly circumstances can guide us. If I receive a letter from the government telling me to pay so many thousand dollars in taxes, circumstances are guiding me to pay. If I am walking in the rain with my umbrella, I am being guided by circumstances to put up my umbrella.

But there are times when circumstances are to be overcome rather than to be given way to. When the Israelites sent spies into the land that God told them to go into, the spies came back and said there were giants. "We're pygmies in their eyes. We can't go in there." Yet God was guiding them; and the circumstances, whatever they were, were circumstances to be overcome. If missionaries were to heed the governments of certain countries and follow circumstances, they would rapidly conclude that God had not guided them to preach the gospel there.

When a door is shut you can do two things. You can say, "Aha! I'm not supposed to go through that door," and you can walk away. Or you can try to open the door. If it is locked, you can knock. If you have a key, you can unlock it. Or you can batter the door down. Circumstances are not the masters of our fate. One of the problems of guidance is to know when circumstances are to be taken to direct us and when they are to be overcome. I'm going to look at this issue in the course of these discussions.

Besides dreams and circumstances, there are also inner promptings. God guides by that deep sense within me that he is leading me in a certain direction. But how can I be sure that the prompting is from God and isn't an unconscious way of doing what I want to do anyway? I don't want to get embroiled in the debate about divorce and remarriage, but as I have counseled people wanting to marry after having been divorced, I have found the way they get guidance a bit suspect. A lot of the time the guidance seems to arise from their desire. If I see a beautiful piece of pie in the refrigerator and I feel hungry, it's easy to get guidance to eat that pie. Frankly, sometimes our desires are behind the guidance. But I must not give the impression that God always guides us to do things we hate! So how do I distinguish between what I want and what is true inner prompting?

The counsel of others presents a similar problem. Certainly much can be said for going to older and wiser people who have faced similar problems and asking their counsel. But counselors can be wrong. There is no perfect counselor. And sometimes I may have to go in the face of the good counsel that is given to me. How can I know?

Sometimes there are prophecies. In charismatic circles Christians wait to hear God speak directly through his people to guide them. Brief prophetic utterances may be directed to a particular member of the congregation. If the prophecy is truly from God, we have sound guidance. But again we're not out of danger. When Paul was being directed by God to go to Jerusalem, every prophecy he encountered said don't go (Acts 21:10-11). It wasn't that the prophecies were wrong. As a matter of fact, they were merely warning him of the horrors to come. But the guidance of God to Paul was that he should go in the face of all the prophecies against the trip.

People also put out fleeces for guidance. They ask for a sign to confirm or reject a certain course of action. "Lord, if you want me to go to church tomorrow, don't let it rain or snow, so I can go in comfort." God has used fleeces (Judg 6:11-40), but in general he uses them for weak people. He also uses them to push people in a certain direction. I would warn against presetting conditions. Our own desires might prejudice the conditions we set so that God's guidance will turn out the way we want.

So these are some of the problems of guidance. Dreams, circumstances, inner promptings, the counsel of others, prophecies and fleeces: what are we to do with them all? How are we to find our way through this mass of options for knowing God's will? I want to mention two principles.

First, God wants to guide us far more than we want to be guided. Dreams and counsel and other things notwithstanding, he is so anxious to guide us that sooner or later he's going to get through to us. He gets his guidance across in spite of our obtuseness and sin. God is concerned about us. He will guide us. Let that be a comfort.

Second, it is far better for God to choose the method of guidance than for us. In his own way, in his own time, he will assure you that it is he, God, who is speaking to you. What about those wrong thoughts in your heart? If God wants to guide you, he'll get through to you—unless you're really determined not to be guided.

Trust in the Lord

This brings me to the key prerequisite of guidance. If I had to choose which prerequisite it was most important to meet before I could know God's will, I would say that yielding everything to God comes first, making sure that he has his way. But I'm afraid that's not number one on God's list. If I am to be guided, I must first have confidence in God. Earlier I quoted James 1:5 about the promise of guidance: "If any of you lacks wisdom, let him ask God, who gives to all men generously and without reproaching, and it will be given him." But James goes on to add a prerequisite to guidance. "But let him ask in faith, with no doubting, for he who doubts is like a wave of the sea that is driven and tossed by the wind" (1:6). God's first prerequisite in Proverbs 3:5-6 is just the same. "Trust in the LORD with all your heart . . . and he will make straight your paths."

God's whole object is to teach us to walk with him, to teach us to have fellowship with him. When he puts a problem in our way, and we don't know which way to turn, God moves us to enter anew into a relationship of trust with him. Can I really say I believe that Jesus rose from the dead if I can't believe that he will guide me about my everyday affairs? The God who raised Christ is the God who has promised to guide me. So I begin with faith.

Trusting in the Lord is not a feeling. When Solomon says, "Trust in the LORD with all your *heart,*" he does not mean emotion or conscience, but will. Trust is a decision. It is coming to God and saying, "Lord, I don't see how you are going to guide me, but I choose to believe that you're going to. I'm going to look to you and you alone for guidance. You are more concerned about this problem than I am. So I have decided to base my future actions on that confidence." Picture an Eskimo who comes to Winnipeg and sees skyscrapers for the first time. You tell him, "Press that button, and you'll go to the fifteenth floor." His feelings may not tell him that he will go to the fifteenth floor. But if he presses the button, he will go. This is like trusting God.

Wanting It All

Lastly we come to the priorities in guidance, God's priorities. Let me state his first priority negatively. God is not interested in guiding us about just one choice. Suppose I say to an interior decorator, "Look at our dining room. It's a mess. Please do something about it."

But the interior decorator might respond, "Your dining

room is a mess. But the problem is that your whole house is a mess. I can't fix the dining room without also dealing with everything that is around it. Give me the whole house to decorate and I'll do the job. But don't ask me to do the dining room alone."

When we come to God asking for guidance, he says, "Give me your life." This is his priority. He does not want to guide us about a specific issue alone. "You have that problem in your life," he says, "because you have not given me the whole of your life. It's not that I can't solve this problem in isolation. It's that the trouble extends to the whole of your life. I want to give your whole life its proper orientation."

He doesn't say this because he is unsympathetic. He cares deeply. Toward the end of *The Magician's Nephew*, Digory is confronted by Aslan.

"Son of Adam," said Aslan. "Are you ready to undo the wrong you have done to my sweet country of Narnia?" . . .

"Yes," said Digory. . . . "But please, please—won't you —can't you give me something that will cure my Mother?" Up till then he had been looking at the Lion's great front feet and the huge claws on them; now, in his despair, he looked up at its face. What he saw surprised him as much as anything in his whole life. For the tawny face was bent down near his own and (wonder of wonders) great shining tears stood in the Lion's eyes. They were such big, bright tears compared with Digory's own that for a moment he felt as if the Lion must really be sorrier about his Mother than he was himself.[1]

We may feel that God doesn't care about our problems, but his heart knows more sorrow than we could ever know. For this very reason he wants to give us the best in all aspects of our being. Following Christ is a lifetime occupation. It's not just going to church and perhaps having a time when you read your Bible each day. Let him lead all that you do.

Long ago people didn't go to a university and take so many credits to get an education. They learned by attaching themselves to a master. They became the disciples of that master. As a matter of fact, they became his personal servant. And in the course of that intimate relationship of servant and master, they learned from him, they were disciplined by him, they were subject to him in all things, and changes took place in them. If I want guidance in my life, I must become that kind of disciple of the Lord Jesus.

Going on a Blind Date

Let me also begin my discussion of God's second priority in guidance by stating it negatively. While he demands the whole of our lives, he will not lay out a plan for the rest of our lives. You say, "How can I commit my life to him when I do not know the details? It's like a blind date. I don't know what he wants and I don't know what I'll get." Indeed it is just that. If I wanted to go to Miami, I could write to an automobile club and they would give me a bunch of papers telling me just how to get there from Winnipeg. They would show me all the main roads and the detours and the alternate routes. All I would do is follow the papers.

God does not give us one of those plans. He doesn't even tell us where we are going. In Genesis 12:1 he tells Abraham, "Go from your country and your kindred and your father's house to the land that I will show you." Abraham knew the direction but not the destination. Yet that was sufficient.

We too can know the direction—holiness. God desires to make us holy. But he will not tell us the details. He will not tell us where we will wind up. We have to trust him for that. The question of guidance thus becomes a question of faith. Can I trust him to take charge of my life and to direct it even when I don't know where it's going? The wonderful thing is that he is worthy of that trust. He is worthy because of his power. He is able to accomplish all things. He is worthy because of his love. He knows our desires and our sorrows. He is worthy.

If God doesn't tell us our final destination, what is the next step we should take? In Psalm 119:105 we read, "Thy word is a lamp to my feet and a light to my path." Some Christians use the Bible for guidance on particular problems. And it is wonderful how sometimes, as we are reading the Scriptures and praying, God may grip us with a passage of Scripture so that he seems to be saying something very specific to us. God certainly does that. But there is danger in saying, "God, I'm going to find a verse in Mark 10, and you're going to tell me what to do through that verse." We can't command God. We're dealing with a loving, personal, sovereign God. When he says his Word is a lamp to our feet, he is referring to the *whole* of Scripture. If our minds were so soaked in Scripture that in any circumstance we knew how it applied, half of our problems in guidance would never occur.

Guidance, you see, is not merely geographical (shall I choose this direction or that?), it is also moral. What is the *right* thing, the upright thing, the godly thing, to do in these circumstances? Admittedly, it is not always easy to do what is right just because I *know* what is right. But I will at least know what choice God wants me to make. That is why Psalm 119:9 and 11 say, "How can a young man keep his way pure? By guarding it according to thy word. . . . I have laid up thy word in my heart, that I might not sin against thee."

Some think that missionaries are special people. Missionaries know where they're going in life. After all, they're called to a specific country. But you ask missionaries and they will tell you that it is not like that at all. They may have headed for one country and wound up in another. They may have thought of one kind of work and ended up doing something entirely different. All of us have the same kind of guidance; all of us are supposed to have a call in life like Abraham's.

Isaiah 30:21 makes the same point. God says to Israel, "Your ears shall hear a word behind you, saying, 'This is the way, walk in it,' when you turn to the right or when you turn to the left." Here God is not primarily concerned with geographical guidance or with learning to do his will. The context of the verse is the moral confusion in Israel: Israel had become idolatrous. They had been told that there was no inconsistency in worshiping idols and worshiping God. They did not know right from wrong. So God promises them a new teacher, God the Holy Spirit, who will teach them what is right in worship.

The people of Israel found comfort in God's promise to guide them into purity. God wants the same for us. He is not concerned that we win a lottery or even that we avoid all pain. But he is concerned that we find wholeness of life—which can only come through him and in accordance with his ways. And we will find comfort in the new and intimate relationship with a Person who is *the* guide in our life, whose walk with us will mean more than anything else in life.

20
The Power
of Forgiveness

_____It was the last thing she had expected.

She had been waiting for death—by stoning. Then, in a way she was at a loss to explain, the accusations ceased to echo from the walls around her. She looked up and discovered the menacing crowd was melting away. At last only One remained.

What now? A cold dismissal? Should she sneak away while she had a chance? Would he say anything? What he did say exploded over her with a power she would never forget.

"Neither do I condemn you; go, and do not sin again" (Jn 8:11).

No power on earth can touch pardon. Atomic power can vaporize a city. It can raise a mushroom cloud miles into the sky. But it can neither soften a hardened heart, straighten the shoulders of a discouraged person nor break the power of sin.

Forgiveness can do all this—and more.

Have you ever watched the face of people who were weighed down by guilt and who realized for the first time that God in Christ had forgiven them? It's unearthly. I saw it when my son was six years old. He had read *Little Pilgrim's Progress* and began to ask me about it. Would Jesus forgive him even if he had been very bad? He would? And wash him white? How white? Whiter than snow? His mouth twisted with longing and his eyes were hungry. "Lord Jesus, I know you know I have been very bad." The knowledge was crushing even to a six-year-old. His head was bowed against my knee. "Please wash my heart in your blood . . ." He looked up and then asked, with a glow in his cheeks, "Is he washing it now, Daddy?"

Christianity is the only religion of forgiveness that exists. Muslims pray, fast, give alms and go on pilgrimages. They neither give nor seek pardon. Allah alone is righteous.

Hindus are caught in the wheel of life. Their sins and their goodness are woven into a future existence as a dog or as a worm. There is no pardon—only endless change from one existence to another. Their only hope is somehow to find release from the wheel of life into nothingness.

The religions of early China that formed Confucius' background offer even less. Their loftiest concept of God is of one who watches and judges. There is no forgiveness—only cold, observant disapproval.

But the coming of Christ shifted the focus to a principle deep in God's heart: the idea of "an eye for an eye" was superseded. God was a God who forgave, freely and completely. The past was to be blotted out.

One purpose of God in forgiving guilty sinners was to start a chain reaction. The forgiven were to forgive. Pardoned sinners were not only to *preach* forgiveness but to *impart* forgiveness for wrongs done to them personally. Forgiveness was more than something to be believed. It was a way of life. "As the Lord has forgiven you, so you also must forgive" (Col 3:13).

So a subtle new power was released among Christian

people. Wherever forgiveness was practiced, a new set of virtues appeared, like flowers that spring up after rainfall in the desert. Gentleness, forbearance and tenderness softened the harsh discords of human relationships. Forgiveness does not only mean to cancel a debt or a punishment. One dictionary I looked up uses the phrase "to cease to feel resentment toward." Forgiveness *restores intimacy*.

Forgiveness does not just let things drift. This is easy to do, easier in fact than to have a terrible fight with whoever wronged you. You press your lips together, shrug your shoulders and say, "The Lord knows." But that isn't forgiveness. To know what forgiveness is, look again at Paul's words, "As the Lord has forgiven you, so you also must forgive." Christ's forgiveness was positive, deliberate and explicit. Ours must be equally so. His forgiveness was complete: he held nothing back. There were no reservations.

Not long ago I was talking to a missionary who had been wronged by another. "Yes, I'll forgive him," the missionary said, "but things can never be the same again." Is that forgiveness? Formal, cold, from behind a closed door? Can you imagine the voice from the throne of Grace saying, "Yes, I will forgive you, but from now on I can't feel the same about you"? Christ's forgiveness doesn't remember. You must have heard more than once, "Yes, I'll forgive, but I'll never forget." To forgive without forgetting is not to forgive at all.

God forgets. "As far as the east is from the west, so far does he remove our transgressions from us" (Ps 103:12). "Thou hast cast all my sins behind thy back" (Is 38:17). "I have swept away your transgressions like a cloud" (Is 44:22). "I will remember [your] sin no more" (Jer 31:34).

When you forgive you must forget too, totally. Blot the thing out of your memory. Put it behind you and keep it there. Do so at once. Christ never waits to forgive.

I find this hard to do. At times when I get mad at my wife,

deep down I know God is not pleased. I know too that I am going to have to forgive her. But I like to hold on a bit. I feel I have a right to a short stretch of sulking. But God wants me to forgive right away, with a smile—and *completely*.

There are problems, of course. Should I forgive my daughter who shows no sign of being sorry? Is not forgiveness conditioned by repentance? In some cases, yes. After all, my relationship with my daughter is a dim reflection of God's relationship with me. In one sense I forgive her before she asks me to. I *offer* forgiveness all the time. But forgiveness is a two-way street. So my daughter can only be said to be forgiven when she sees her need of forgiveness and admits her wrong.

This is why we should go to fellow Christians who have wronged us. Jesus' instructions in Matthew 18 were not to give us a legal weapon to use against someone who hurts us. We approach a brother who has wronged us *because we want to forgive him.* We cannot bear the estrangement the wrong has caused. If he doesn't acknowledge his wrong, he cannot of course accept our forgiveness. (Who wants to be forgiven for something he is not guilty of?) The whole point of church discipline is to keep erring brothers and sisters within the forgiven, forgiving community, not to "put them in their place" or to "show them where to get off." And if all measures fail, our hearts still must bear no resentment.

There are strong links between God's forgiveness of us and our willingness to forgive others. For one thing, our willingness to forgive is a test of whether we are really forgiven. If I am forgiven I will want to forgive. I will go on forgiving because I will discover the joy of what forgiveness does both to me and to the people I forgive.

So if I don't feel like forgiving, there is a reason. Perhaps I have never been forgiven by God. Or else his forgiveness is no longer real to me. I have forgotten the wonder of it. I need to get alone with the Word of God and let the Holy

Spirit teach it to me afresh.

But more than this, forgiveness determines the day-by-day relationship between God our heavenly Father and us his children. "If you do not forgive men their trespasses, neither will your Father forgive your trespasses" (Mt 6:15). If we don't forgive, we will not be forgiven. There is no question of law and grace. Christ is not dealing with the relationship between God the Judge and his creatures, but between God the heavenly Father and us his regenerate children. It is a matter of things going wrong *in the family circle*. As long as we remain unforgiving, our communion with our Father will be broken. We have dammed the stream that was meant to flow to us and through us.

It is a psychological as well as a spiritual fact that unforgiveness produces changes in us. When we don't forgive, we grow plagued by guilt about our own wrongs. God's forgiveness even *seems* unreal. As an old Puritan writer says: "He who will not forgive destroys a bridge which he himself would like to cross."

Have you sensed a block in your prayer life? Could this be the cause? It's a terrible thought, but it should be faced. Your heavenly Father may be unable to forgive you because your heart is too hard and unforgiving. But begin to forgive and you will find yourself changing. You will discover a new tenderness toward the Holy Spirit, a new softness in your heart. You will lose your hard shell. You will experience simple Christian joy.

But forgiveness will do more. It has the power to change the lives of people around us. Only because God has forgiven us can we live holy lives. Being forgiven provides a wonderful incentive to righteousness. Nothing is more deadly than to live in an atmosphere of condemnation. When we sense other people's criticism of us, we make mistakes all the more. On the other hand, a kindly, forgiving attitude brings out the best in us.

Ever been hungry for forgiveness? If so, you will have some idea of the glorious power that is in your own hands. Around you are people whose lives could be changed by your forgiveness. They are waiting for the kindly touch of it now. Give your husband the forgiveness he longs for. Seal it with a kiss, a smile and an extra-nice supper. Give your wife a bunch of flowers. Be forgiving with friends, coworkers and the children, with neighbors and with hypocritical people in church.

Your local spiritual desert will blossom like a rose, and a freshness will come to your own heart that you have not known for many a year.

21
Parrot
Fish

_____They say you get to see spiders and little red snakes. Or tiny green men six inches tall. I saw parrot fish. What's more, I heard them.

I gotta quit, that's all there is to it. I shake so bad in the morning that I can hardly get the bottle to my lips. And sometimes the bottle's already empty.

You know, I've quit twice already—seven months the first time, three the second. So I can do it if I really try. But it's my nerves. If only that fool doctor could sort out my nerves, I'd never touch another drop. I'm no alcoholic, though I admit I've got a problem.

Matter of fact, I can't stand the booze here in Jamaica. Rum. Foul stuff. I just hold my nose and swallow it.

See, I got this job teaching scuba diving to tourists. You don't really teach 'em anything—just watch so they don't get into trouble. Afterward they treat you in the bar . . .

I got a little something in my room too. It's against hotel regulations for the staff, but I got one bottle in the flush tank above the toilet, plus a large after-shave bottle and a largish cologne bottle. Sounds pretty sneaky, but it's the only way I can get to sleep.

But these fish. Parrot fish ten feet long! I know it sounds crazy, and that's what has me scared. But I know a parrot fish when I see one, though these were the first that ever talked.

The thing about going below is the silence, know what I mean? Well, the silence is no more. This time the crazy things talked—booming, screeching parrot-fish talk through echoing waters. You can't scream under water, but I screamed inside my guts.

There was this woman parrot fish with glasses on. "Convention? I defy convention! I intend to be free," she screeched.

The silence came again. None of them seemed to notice me. As the moments passed my heart beat less fiercely. Dim green water and bubbles. Then I jumped like a thousand needles were being pushed through my skin as a professor fish squeaked, "And what do you mean by *free*? No." The lady parrot fish was about to interrupt. "No. Let me make my question clear. In concrete terms, what do you want to be free to do?"

The other fish opened their great mouths and closed them again. The female's eyes narrowed, like she could tell he was still a momma's boy. She began to talk coldly. "Take the surface above us—this silly, wavy, inconsistent plane. Who in Neptune's name decreed that we must always stay below it? Who's to say what is moral and what is immoral? Don't interrupt me till I finish! The thing our ancestors were pleased to call the surface of the ocean is no moral absolute but an arbitrary line established by custom and prejudice. It's not real. In some cultures the line to which we attach such importance is completely ignored. How can I possibly harm anyone by crossing it if I want to? Humans go above and below it. Their morality permits it. And flying fish . . ."

A chorus of protest rose at the mention of flying fish. Words like *flippies, commufish,* the *bomb, fishist,* the *effluvient society* and *extreme right-fin politics* battered my ears and befuddled my brain. Some fish paled visibly.

I got scared. Not 'cause the arguments were any good, but because the fish were so mad. They fought with words like drunks fight with broken beer bottles. They were carving one another up. No one was listening. They were so mad they didn't care whether they hurt or got hurt. It was a brawl in a bar. You could almost see the smashed mirrors, the wrecked chairs, the filth.

It quieted down after a while, and one of the younger fish said, "I like this freedom bit. Like you say, the thing is not to hurt anybody. And if nobody else gets hurt, why not do what you like?"

The younger fish seemed to like this.

The professor and the female with glasses began to speak at the same time. The female won out, which was a pity since she just liked to grab the scene.

"I went on the beach last night."

There were gasps of admiration.

"And I ate with a knife and fork."

"With knife and fork ... !" " ... and fork!" " ... and fork!" echoed among the coral.

"Why not?"

"Sure, why not?" echoed the younger fish who liked the freedom idea.

"Humans do," she continued.

"What are forks?" asked a very young fish, amid general snickers from the preadolescents and serious looks from their elders. "Don't laugh at her," said the female with glasses. "We were all green once. They're plastic things, dear, with four sharp spines you can stick your fins into. They're designed for pushing food into your mouth."

The female had everyone's ear.

"What sort of food?"

"Oh, potato chips and paper . . ."

"Highly indigestible, I would have thought," the professor-type piped.

"Delicious," the female chirped. (Nobody was really in a position to disagree.) "And anyway, I was free. I didn't have to be bound by water. I refuse to spend the rest of my life restricted by the confines of the puny ocean. I refuse to be forced always to suck insipid seafood through my mouth. What's more, I had an experience on the beach that changed my whole life."

A pause ensued, which the female enjoyed for as long as she dared; then, "I laid eggs on the sand."

For a moment, everything stood still. I felt shocked myself, though I don't know why. Neither sound nor movement broke the tension until one fish said softly, "Neptune, I feel sick. You gotta draw the line somewhere. Oh, Neptune . . ." Slowly he turned and swam away into the shadows. The rest stayed on, nervous and jittery.

The young fish who liked freedom said, "I'm not shocked. The ocean's changed in the last ten years. We can't live in the past. We may not always be right, but at least we're not hypocrites, pretending to follow standards we see no sense in. We gotta find out what we really want. We're free."

A fancy pastor-type drifted into the center, cleared his throat, and said, "Some interesting issues have been raised (indeed, I might say, provocative and challenging issues). The whole discussion has been conducted on a mature and responsible level. Personally, I feel I've learned a great deal. Though I'm not certain what advantages there were to laying eggs on sand." He seemed to think he was being funny and the professor smiled and nodded. "It is perhaps inconsistent with our concept of Neptune to think of the matter in outmodedly rigid terms. There is nothing sinful about laying eggs. There is nothing bad about sand. And it might be, under certain circumstances, a very meaningful thing to do to lay eggs on sand. After all, freedom is Neptune's gift to us."

Maybe my head was clearing. At any rate, the fish were returning to their normal size. One old parrot fish, who seemed to shrink more slowly than the rest, was staring me right in the eye, never moving a fin. He was the first to notice me, and as I stared back he winked, ever so slowly.

I winked back. I wasn't sure what we were winking about, but I didn't want to offend him. Anyway, I was still scared.

"Freedom," he said contemptuously. "Freedom is doing what you were made to do and doing it with all you've got."

The rest of the fish had disappeared, and the old fish himself was growing smaller. I wanted to ask him more, but there was no time. Yet he still held my eye and his voice was powerful and strong. "Knives and forks! Potato chips!" His scorn made me cringe. "Watch!"

It was the last word I heard. He turned in a flash and was sliding through blue-green water, hovering, twisting, darting, gliding. Four other fish joined him in the frolic, their movements one, as though I had quintuple vision. Each twist was clean and perfectly timed. I was watching a ballet so taut and sharp that the toughest discipline on earth would never reproduce it. Yet suddenly I knew I was watching freedom. Freedom for fish.

But for me? The pressure in my tank was down, and I began to think of the bottle of rum in the flush tank of my bathroom. I turned for home.

So freedom is doing what you were made to do, and doing it with all you've got. What was I made to do? I felt freest when I had three or four ounces of hard liquor inside me. Free from the ugliness of reality. Were feeling free and being free the same? After all, what was I made for?

It was worth a second thought—maybe even a sober thought.

22
Priscilla
and Apollos

They drifted through the doorway in tittering huddles, clinging shyly to one another. The matron of the Internado, a privately run hostel for women students, had rounded them up, shooing them from all parts of the conventlike building into the sala. They all offered us their hands with bashful politeness, so that I felt now a clammy palm, now a warm one, in my own.

"Mucho gusto . . ."

"Maria Suarez para servirle . . ."

"Mucho gusto!"

"Mucho gusto!"

More titters. Congestion round the doorway. We backed to make room.

Someone said, "Please sit down." So Mim Lemcke and I sat on erect wooden chairs. It felt like being enthroned and receiving an audience, for everyone else remained standing in the large room, staring at us and giggling whenever our glances crossed theirs.

It was an odd situation. Earlier that evening, Juan, a student, had met us by appointment outside Toluca University

(Mexico). As so often happens, the rest of the student group that was to have met us had not shown up. At the entrance to the university our pale skins had invited curious stares, but Juan had seemed unconcerned. Then it had begun to rain.

"Let's go over to the Internado," Juan had said. "Some of the girls from there promised to come. They're probably still over there."

"What about the students coming to meet us here?" I objected.

"Alfredo will look after them," he said.

He had piloted us through the rain to a drab colonial building down a narrow street. I had felt ill at ease standing in the rain outside the big wooden door, wondering whether the matron of the Internado would be puzzled and even embarrassed by the sudden, unannounced arrival of foreigners representing an unknown Christian organization. Juan had not shared my doubts, nor were his spirits dampened by the rain. He had explained that in the curious old building lived thirty señoritas who studied at the Normal School and University of Toluca. The door opened in response to our knocking, and we were welcomed inside.

In a kind of dream, Mim and I had found ourselves being introduced to the matron, exchanging polite platitudes about the "vital strategic nature" and the "tremendous responsibilities" of her work and ours. Moments later, in the sala, we had been swamped with the deluge of giggling girls.

And now we sat and stared. They stood and stared. You can't really preach to a standing congregation when you've just been asked to sit down. In fact we hadn't come to preach. I wasn't very clear why we had come or what to do next.

Only Juan seemed totally at ease. He cut a fine if slightly sleek figure, his round young face heavy with solemnity. He cleared his throat and began to speak, emphasizing his well-turned phrases by waving a pudgy hand.

We all represented youth, he said, and youth was vital. Youth was dynamic. We lived in an atomic age, and we should be full of, er, of explosions—like atoms. Christianity was not a matter for long faces. Christianity was . . .

The girls were electrified, and I wished I hadn't come. What next? The matron's eyes had a worried look. I didn't dare look at Mim.

Juan wasn't finished. In fact, he began to improve.

He talked about the need to evangelize the university. This was a job for students. If the señoritas felt scared, they must realize that it wasn't *they* who were to do the work, but Christ in them. Suddenly it dawned on me that I wasn't really listening to Juan at all. I was listening to Mim Lemcke. And Mim, sitting on a wooden chair, was pressing her lips together and looking haunted.

But it was Mim all right. Mim's ideas (even Mim's catch-words) being spouted in fluent Spanish by smooth, irrepressible, impeccable young Juan, with his dark suit, his Yardley's-cologne smell and his two imitation black pearl pins. The introduction was Juan's but the rest was pure Lemcke.

He talked about quiet times; about group Bible study; about the need to testify; about how to get cracking. There was a bit more about exploding atoms and long faces, but mostly it was terrific. And Juan seemed to mean it.

How in the world had she done it? I recalled Mim's telling me about a trip she had made with Juan. "I tried to get across to him . . . I tried to show him . . . I talked to him about . . ." Seemed that something had registered.

The gathering was ballooning into a full-scale meeting. The señoritas sat down. Embarrassment was evaporating (though Juan had really never had any). He was like Apollos, the eloquent Jew from Alexandria whose teaching was good but had not included the full gospel message (Acts 18:24-28). Apolloses will spout eloquent piffle or eloquent sense, according to whether they have run into and been redirected and corrected by some modern Priscilla or Aquila.

The rest of the meeting went superbly. Cards were passed around and the girls signed their names, together with a note of the day and time when they wanted their meetings.

I don't know what will come of that meeting in Toluca. I don't even know what will become of Juan. How can you tell in advance how anyone is going to turn out? The brightest prospects sputter into silence like damp firecrackers, while unlikely candidates do great exploits. You can never tell.

But if Mim continues her Operation Priscilla, one day she will hit a real Apollos—a person Mexico needs badly for Christian ministry. With Juan it may have been just a spark in the night. Yet even if it was, I have seen in the light of the flash the startling glory of what God can do through a Priscilla in the life of an Apollos.

Part IV
Problems of
Christian
Discipleship

23
Self—The Unjolly Giant

_____Promotion brings him no happiness. The higher his salary, the more money he craves. The more friends he has, the more he yearns for friendship. The more his friends praise him, the more worried he grows about what they really think of him.

If his Sunday-school class shows enthusiasm for his lesson, he enjoys satisfaction but only briefly. If he is a pastor, the response from his congregation never quite satisfies him. He yearns for heartier "Amens!" and ever larger churches. He is driven to greater efforts in a feverish desire for deeper appreciation.

Every day he carries a burden of debilitating discontent. No sooner does he bite into attractive fruit than he finds it tasteless. Nothing pleases him. He is like the man of whom Montague Goodman said, "He does what he likes, but he doesn't *like* what he *does*."

His problem is self.

Not Gold but Chains of Gold
What is self? Self is at once a principle, a power and a monster that devours. It is a life principle that governs our be-

havior. It profoundly affects our attitudes and actions. Self is the principle in me that says, "Whatever else happens, I must make sure I make out O.K. I must see that all my needs are met and my interests provided for. I must try to have people think well of me."

Now the hardest question to answer is this: Why should such a principle exist in the life of a Christian at all, when God is deeply concerned that his children enjoy the very best? "My God," Paul writes, "will supply every need of yours" (Phil 4:19).

Nowhere does the Bible teach that we can please God more by eating less or wearing shoes with bigger holes. "Consider the lilies of the field," Jesus once said, " . . . I tell you, even Solomon in all his glory was not arrayed like one of these" (Mt 6:28-29). As a matter of fact, God is delighted to give us more than we need. He is not stingy. He does not measure out his blessings parsimoniously, for there is no shortage. Space and time are crammed with all he has to offer us.

Nor is it correct to say that spiritual blessings and material blessings are governed by different laws, and that we have to be poor materially in order to be rich spiritually. This is simply not true. Poor Christians, as a class, are not more spiritually blessed than Christians who have everything. Missionaries with tiny allowances do not necessarily enjoy more heavenly riches than their well-endowed colleagues. In fact, some of the poorer missionaries are so busy trying not to feel sore about the way they have to scrimp that they have no heart left to relish heavenly joys.

The fact is that God wants our lives to turn out in the best possible way. He wants us to be filled with joy, and insofar as marriage, career or ambitions will contribute to such full-ness of joy, he wants these things for us too.

God doesn't want to rescue us from earthly joys so much as from bondage to earthly joys. It is bondage that hinders blessing just as it is bondage that is the mark of the self principle. God wants to rescue us, not from gold but from chains of gold. Then why, if God wants the very best spiritually, materially and intellectually for us all, should the self principle even exist? Why, indeed?

Part of the answer lies in the words of my definition, *"I must make sure."* The words imply two things: first, *I* am to be the one who makes decisions (*I* must make sure); second, there is some doubt (hence the need to *make sure*) about the way things may turn out if . . . if what? If God is left to look after things!

Self has its deepest roots in doubt. We doubt that God's ideas as to what is best for us are to be trusted. We are not sure how effective he'll be in coping. He may be God, but, after all, one has to use a bit of common sense . . .

I cannot place too much emphasis on explaining the exact nature of the self principle. If you go away from this feeling that self is the same as wanting something for yourself, I shall have failed in my task. For it is not wrong to hunger or to crave sleep; to want sex or more money; to want pretty things or to be ambitious. All these longings can, in themselves, be legitimate. Only when, because of fear and doubt, my wants fill the horizon, or my ambitions become my main reason for living; only when I begin to say (though perhaps in a voice so low that I fail to hear myself say it), *"I must make sure* I get what I want," does self become my problem. And at that point it becomes a problem too tough for me to handle.

Self is a power as well as a principle, a power that dominates our minds, our feelings and our actions. Try as we will, we cannot shake it off.

Some people, excessively zealous to overcome self, have adopted the unhappy religious principle of trampling underfoot every bodily and mental desire, confusing desire with the self principle itself. They have starved themselves,

chosen poverty needlessly, humiliated themselves to conquer their pride and ambition—only to find that they have
gone on craving food (or sleep or sex), gone on being proud
(about their humility), gone on struggling to bridge bottom-
less chasms of envy. After years of conflict they have discovered that, though the ground of the battle against self
may have shifted, the power of self is undiminished.

Cuckoo in the Sparrow's Nest

In one sense it would be more accurate to describe self as a
monster rather than as a power. Self has a voracious appetite, an unquenchable thirst. It demands that we get from
other people a never-ending supply of praise, admiration,
comfort, courtesy, affection, understanding (it's unbeliev-
ably touchy), to mention but a few.

And I am the person who has to see that it get these. Give
self an inch and it'll scream for a mile. The more it has, the
more it demands, until my life becomes the life of the man
described at the beginning of this chapter, the harassed and
haunted slave of illusions.

Self is like the cuckoo. Cuckoos lay their eggs in other
birds' nests. A baby cuckoo in a sparrow's nest may be three
times the size of its foster parents. I will never forget the
comic-tragic sight of a pair of hedge sparrows, frantically
darting to and from their nest to supply an enormous baby
cuckoo with bits of food. It amazed me to see what power
the cuckoo held to keep the sparrows on the move. His lusty
cries could be heard for a quarter of a mile. The sparrows
had grown thin and weary in their endless haste to cram
food into his insatiable gullet.

Self is a cuckoo in the nest of your heart. Like the sparrows, you are driven mercilessly by his cries to be satisfied.
And the bigger he gets, the hungrier he grows; while the
hungrier he grows, the louder he shrieks.

But there's another aspect to the problem. So long as the

cuckoo in the nest gets preference, the weak cries of the baby sparrows are less effective in securing food from their parents. In the same way, so long as the strident voice of self enslaves you, the real you, the redeemed you, the new creation in Christ, will have little chance to grow. You'll be too busy feeding self.

How did we get to be saddled with a cuckoo? Where did the monster come from?

Self is that within us which defied and still defies the sanctifying lordship of Christ. Self is that part of us that still wants to run our lives. And because self is astute, it has fooled us into believing it can give us a better deal than Christ. In fact, it is subtler still: Self fools us into believing that it is us—and that we are the ones in control.

But are we? The theory holds no water, theologically or practically. After all, we are the ones being run ragged. Self is the creature crying for more food. Of course, if we submit to its cries, if we identify with it, go along with its plans, then I suppose there is a sense in which we become one with the self.

As God sees it, however, the real me is the redeemed me. What Christ redeemed included my very core, and having freed it he gave me liberty to choose whom I would serve (see Rom 6:12-14). The whole point is that before being redeemed I had no choice but to be errand boy to a cuckoo. Having been redeemed, I have the power to choose.

So notice the change. Formerly we were slaves because we couldn't help ourselves. "You who were once slaves of sin" (Rom 6:17). Now (if Christ really has redeemed us) we are either free indeed or slaves by choice. We don't have to spend the rest of our days feeding a cuckoo, for we are under no obligation to it whatsoever!

Heaving Out the Monster

Admittedly, like the sparrows, we have a problem. The

ideal solution would have been for them to tip the fat intruder out of the nest. But how? Easy enough if one is big and strong, but for tiny sparrows there were two difficulties.

There was first the sheer matter of size. Both sparrows together weighed less than their foster child. But this was not the greatest problem. The heart of the matter lay in the racket the little monster was making. There was something so plaintive, so infinitely moving, so compelling about it that the sparrows couldn't resist him. I doubt if at that stage they had even thought of tipping him out of the nest. When the cuckoo squawked, the sparrows simply flew.

Similar problems beset self-ridden Christians. Self-pity cries compellingly for satisfaction. Self's plea for praise and admiration is hard to resist. The clamor of unsatisfied self makes every fiber of our beings vibrate with the desire to give our cuckoo what it wants. Self cries, "Pity me!" and we cannot resist. Or, if our eyes are opened to our wretchedness, where will we get the strength to heave out the monster we've been fattening so long?

The first step is to be honest. Who, in fact, runs your life? Does the self principle? Are you fattening a cuckoo? Take time for a prayerful survey, asking the Holy Spirit for an answer in the light of God's Word. Go over this chapter again. If any verses of Scripture occur to you, look them up and think about them. Let God show you your true situation.

The second step must be one of repentance; and in repenting we will need to do more than merely feel a tinge of remorse about the way things are. We may regret we are slaves to self, but regret and repentance are not the same. We must admit to ourselves and to God that we have cheated Christ out of his place in our hearts. Self has been ruling where he should have control. The long series of small decisions by which we supplanted Christ and gave power to self were our decisions. We are responsible, not just for our present plight, but for pushing Christ to one side. A thousand times over we chose to please self and to forget Christ. After admitting it, we are prepared to give Christ his place.

The third step is one of faith. We may not feel free, but nevertheless Christ, by his blood, has made us free. (The sparrows don't have to feed the cuckoo—they only *think* they have to!) Faith is not a matter of feelings, and it does not consist in changing feelings. Rather it is more a matter of seeing things the way God sees them, the way they really are. And we really are free!

Notice, however, the nature of our freedom. It is not freedom to overcome or destroy self so much as freedom to choose between Christ and self, at any given time. We may choose a greater power or a lesser, a sanctifying Presence or a defiling passion. And our choice will always be respected. As we choose correctly, the purer voice will steadily increase to drown out the impure. It is not we who conquer self, but Christ.

The fourth step is not so much a step as a walk—a long series of steps of faith, of daily choices, by which we, of our own free(d) will, acknowledge Christ as Master instead of self. With every such step we declare ourselves to be part and parcel of Calvary and the empty tomb. And with every such step the clamor of self will lessen and its bondage melt away, replaced by the joy and freedom of the Lord of glory.

24
Deadly
Depression

_____In a way it is like being seasick. All you want to do is crawl into bed and die. You don't want to eat; you don't want to move; you don't want to talk (especially to bright, cheerful people, the vinegar-to-the-teeth variety). But while seasickness is soon over on a modern voyage, being depressed can go on a long time. Some people grow into permanent Jonahs.

This is tragic. When Jesus said, "Blessed are those who mourn," he did not mean, "Blessed are the discouraged," for discouragement is deadly. It not only depresses you, but it puts you in neutral, spiritually speaking. It stunts or stops your spiritual growth and service.

More important, it affects other people. Ever noticed how a canary stops singing when you put a cloth over its cage? Well, some Christians are like a canary cloth—song stiflers. At times I have been one of them. A heavy pall of gloom chokes out all joy. You can almost see it settling over people, snuffing out smiles like so many flickering candle flames.

"I Quit!"

It destroys many hours of service. "I quit!" cry discouraged ministers in disgust. And, as they get to brooding (which is what you do when you have time on your hands), they begin to see that they should have quit long ago. In fact, it was a mistake to start at all. Whereas optimists do the impossible by their cheerful refusal to take reality too seriously, pessimists (and you are always a pessimist when you are fed up) cannot even do the possible because of their refusal to see it *is* possible. And then begins the descending spiral. The more inactive they become, the more disgusted with themselves they grow. The more disgusted they are, the less they feel they can do anything. And so it goes on.

Most important of all, discouragement offends God. At least it does when we hug it to our bosoms for comfort. It is sin to give his loving Spirit the cold shoulder and nurse an attack of the blues. I don't mean that God fails to understand or pity. He does care. "He knows our frame; he remembers that we are dust" (Ps 103:14). In fact if I knew my frame and remembered that I am dust, I wouldn't get knocked out so easily by discouragement.

Discouragement can be partly physical. I may be overworked or short of sleep. I may have digestive trouble or anemia. I may even have a depressive illness caused by a chemical imbalance in my blood, requiring expert medical attention (see *The Masks of Melancholy*). I don't mean that these things are excuses for sulking. But it is a help to know that depression may come from physical causes since sometimes we fear that something much deeper has gone wrong. We are dust. God put us in bodies, and we are to some extent at their mercy. Instead of telling ourselves that we must have committed some unpardonable sin, it might be good to ask such questions as: How many hours sleep did I have last night? How long since I took a good day off? What kind of food have I been eating lately?

There are other elements, of course. Just as certain insane people go through a regular cycle of wild, manic excitement and profound depression, so all of us go through the same cycle on a milder scale. Sometimes we sparkle. Sometimes we go flat. When we're down, things just don't look so encouraging. If such a period coincides with a reversal at work or a spiritual failure, then watch out! The stage is set for discouragement.

Satan's Strategy

There are spiritual reasons too. Satan won't pass up a chance to make the most of our discouragement. If we are mainly discouraged about ourselves, he will play the accuser. He will show us as we really are. He does not have to exaggerate. We writhe in horrid fascination, groaning as we see the real, disgusting, despicable persons we are.

If, on the other hand, we are mainly discouraged about the way other people (or even God) have been letting us down, he will play the Great Sympathizer. "You sure have had it tough. There *are* limits to human endurance. You always did have a nervous temperament anyway. One can only take so much but no more!" By the time he has finished, we are not only discouraged. We are wallowing in misery and liking it.

Notice his strategy. He doesn't mind if we look at circumstances or at other people or even at ourselves. He does object if we look at God.

By all means we should take a look at ourselves. But we must remember that Christ loves us knowing just what we are. What is more, however rotten our core, we are still in Christ. We must therefore study ourselves in context. The depression we feel springs from mortification. We want to be something in ourselves rather than in Christ.

With Satan's skilled manipulation, discouragement becomes an enervating luxury. Like the Englishman, we are never so happy as when we are miserable. We cuddle into an emotional ball, blanketed by misery, our feet on hot-water bottles of self-pity. And the worst is that we feel either that we have every right to do so, or else that we are being "humble" or "realistic."

Take Elijah, for example. After being tremendously useful and winning exciting victories (always a time to anticipate an attack of the blues), he says: "It is enough; now, O LORD, take away my life; for I am no better than my fathers." Stage 1: self-disgust.

God does not approve. He does take pity, however. He remembers Elijah's physical condition and gives him food and rest. Later Elijah says: "I have been very jealous for the LORD, the God of Hosts; . . . and I, even I only, am left; and they seek my life, to take it away" (see 1 Kings 19). This is Stage 2: self-pity.

It Isn't Easy

Easy to recognize, isn't it? But not so easy to lick! If it was a big thing for Elijah, it will be a big thing for us. If God took it seriously and sympathetically in Elijah's case, he will do the same in ours.

But I don't want to make it sound easy, for discouragement can be the very reverse. Sometimes it presses in like a great physical weight. No one detests more than I the silly, peppy song leader who wags his finger roguishly, flashes his white teeth and says, "Now, where are those smiles? Christians are happy people! A lot of people I can see tonight don't look like Christians at all! That's better! Amen! *Now . . .*" You know the patter.

If it were as easy as that, spiritual giants would have no difficulty. Yet the majority of renowned servants of the Lord, as Spurgeon once pointed out, have had tremendous battles with discouragement and depression. I used to whistle when I was a Scout and I still try singing, but sometimes I have to sing through clenched teeth. If men like John Bun-yan, David Brainerd and the prophet Elijah wrestled in agony with discouragement, it will take more than song-leader patter to help us. More significant, it is only as we learn to battle fiercely against our inner despairing that we will turn from a spiritual child into a mature man or woman of God. There are no short cuts to spiritual maturity.

What can we do to deal with depression?

Praise in the Darkness

The first question to ask about discouragement is, Do I *want* to deal with it? Or would I rather sit down and wait to see whether it will go away by itself? How do I look at discour-agement? As a friend? As a trial? Or as an enemy? We make a big mistake if we adopt a passive attitude about it. Dis-couragement is an enemy that has no right to impose on us. The first step is to be honest about this, and by faith to put our passive attitude aside. It means getting up and tackling our depression, kicking away the hot-water bottle and throwing the blankets of misery out the window! Hard? Of course it is! It is like getting out of bed on a cold, dark morn-ing—only much worse. But it can be done.

Try the Paul-and-Silas method (see Acts 16:25). Sing in the dark. Remember what I said about singing through clenched teeth? Maybe Paul and Silas began their songfest that way. Perhaps it was only as they began to realize the glory of the Lord that the real praise came bubbling through. And then came the earthquake and light in the darkness.

My wife and I tried this once when we were too depressed to pray together. We did not actually sing, but we praised. We wrote down on a piece of paper all the items we had to praise God for, including our few material possessions (we were poor at the time and lived with our baby in one room with a few bits and pieces). The list soon grew to be surprisingly long; so we divided it into groups of five items and took turns praising God. We praised him for the mat on the floor; we praised him for our two pink sheets, our linen tablecloth, our plastic dishes, our alarm clock, our socks and our underwear. The more we praised, the richer we felt. By the time we came to the spiritual blessings, we were burning with joy and satisfaction.

Or try the Habakkuk technique. "Though the fig tree do not blossom . . ." (Hab 3:17-19). How might it go in modern English? "Although the international situation is appalling and I face real losses in business; even though my wife [or husband] fails to understand me and my home is full of problems; though Christian friends let me down and Christian work reveals its seamy side; worst of all, though I get to know the real me: *yet will I rejoice in the LORD!* I will joy in the God of my salvation; the Lord God is my strength, and he will make me to walk on my high places." Amen. May it be so. The Bible does not tell us to rejoice in ourselves or our circumstances, or our feelings. All of these are changeable and will let us down. We are to rejoice in the Lord—in who he is, what he has done, and what he is doing.

Does it still feel impossible to overthrow discouragement? Is our situation too hopeless to admit a ray of light? Read the following words of Marshall Foch from a cable to Paris while he was facing almost certain defeat during World War 1: "My center gives way; my right retreats. Situation excellent. I attack." It is not the situation that matters but what we do about it. And if a French general in impossible difficulties could react as he did, how much more can we!

25
The
Gossip
Within

_____It's one of those tiny but disastrous things like termites in the rafters, a crack in a dam, a lighted cigarette tossed into a pine forest. Gossip shatters friendships, ruins marriages, breaks hearts, disrupts churches. And it is a problem that seems to be growing in Christian circles.

There are times when it is necessary to talk about someone's failings. The committee that has to decide whether I should be given a certain job, for instance, might have to talk about my bad points as well as my good points. If it does its duty, it will go into some areas of my life pretty thoroughly. But members of the committee will only be backbiting if they do so because they enjoy it, or if they chat with their spouses about my faults when the committee meeting is over.

The Blunt and the Subtle

We can practice the fine art of gossip in several ways. If we are not very expert, we can adopt the candid, blunt technique. We can say, "I don't have much use for Brother Brown," and then give the reasons. We don't hide our dislike; we might even add, "And I'd say so to his face!" This may not hoodwink anyone, but it sounds good.

Or we can be more subtle—a help in easing our consciences if God has been speaking to us about gossip. We can say, "Yes, she *is* a nice girl. Pity about her habit of . . ." and then spend ten minutes running her down in a kindly sort of way.

The pseudospiritual approach offers variety. It might begin, "Mary needs our prayers. She has problems with her temper." Then follows a thorough analysis of Mary's spiritual weaknesses, so that others can pray "more intelligently" about it, later on.

We can pull someone to pieces with pious platitudes. Pastors and preachers are particularly easy meat. We can discuss their preaching, their wives, their children. If they dress badly, we can ask what kind of testimony they think it is to go round looking like tramps. If they dress nicely, we can wonder (aloud) where they get the money. The important thing, of course, is to make it clear it is the *testimony* we are worried about.

But whether the approach is direct or more subtle and oblique—wrapped in layers of pious phrases—backbiting is still backbiting. Beneath its apparent triviality lurks danger. The Bible places a gossip in the same bracket as an alcoholic. Titus 2:3 bids the older women "not to be slanderers or slaves to drink." In Paul's mind the one seems as bad as the other.

Disparaging others does the devil's work for him. He is the "accuser of the brethren." Gossip is even more effective when it walks about disguised as an angel of light.

When we put down someone, we not only create tragedy for others. We make difficulties for ourselves in at least two ways. First, others lose confidence in us. Second, we become abnormally conscious of how others may be criticizing *us*. We become extrasensitive to other people's opinions.

I was very fond (and still am) of a Christian worker who was always talking to me about the failures of other members of the group with whom we worked. My conscience protested, but I joined in the conversation. By the time I had known my friend three months, I had learned of the weaknesses of practically every other member of the team.

I don't remember when it began, but after a while I started feeling uneasy in my friend's presence. If he pulled other people to pieces when talking to me, did he pull *me* to pieces when talking to them? One day I discovered that he did. His criticisms of me, given me secondhand, shook me. Fortunately we were able to discuss the problem frankly, and we both learned a useful lesson. But often no such happy solution comes about. The intimacy established as two friends pull their acquaintances apart proves illusory. And, in time, it gives place to mutual distrust.

The Lure of Gossip

Why do we gossip? Because too often we find it enjoyable to learn about and discuss people's faults. "The words of a whisperer are like delicious morsels" (Prov 26:22). The press discovered this long ago. Scandal makes news. As a British press lord put it rather crudely, "There's money in muck."

If we want to get at the root of the problem of criticism in Christian circles, we must ask ourselves *why* we criticize and gossip. What makes it so enjoyable? Obviously it goes back beyond lips. Critical words always come from a critical heart. "Out of the abundance of the heart his mouth speaks" (Lk 6:45). If we are full of critical feelings toward other people, we won't be able to stop putting these feelings into words.

Bitter feelings may not be involved. Faultfinding may be just a pleasant diversion or an ingrained habit. The point is, whatever is in our minds is what we talk about.

Some people criticize others because they flatter themselves that they are good judges of character. If Penelope (who is discerning) analyzes her friends' characters with Grace (who judges character even more discerningly), it is surprising how much human weakness—real or imaginary —they will discover between them. And in doing so their self-importance will receive a big boost. So beware of that ability to assess character. It has its dangers.

Another thing that will lure us inevitably into a gossip-gabble is listening to gossip. If we listen, we have to start contributing sooner or later. Before we realize it, we're apt to get in at the kill. Sometimes, too, it's like telling jokes. We have to tell one that's bigger.

An unconscious sense of our own failings and shortcomings will also make us want to criticize other people. Pulling others to pieces will make us feel better about ourselves. We begin to feel we're not so bad after all.

It's rather like the mental mechanism that makes me enjoy the naughtiness in other people's children. Staying with friends a short time ago, I noticed a strained expression on my hostess's face as her two-year-old acted up. Finally she said, "You must think Tommy's awfully badly behaved. He's not usually quite as bad as this."

"Not at all," I replied, hiding my joy with effort. I could afford to be gracious. I was luxuriating in the relief of knowing that my own children must be pretty normal.

It's the same—but much more dangerous—in the case of criticizing others. We are trying to pull the people we criticize down below our own level. And we'll be all the more likely to do this if we're jealous of the person in question.

The love for creating a sensation also makes us gossip. Have you ever stumbled across a bit of devastatingly scandalous news about an important figure in somebody else's church—the kind of thing that calls for gasps and tut-tuts? You could just imagine how people would react and how important you, the newsbearer, would become. And the more you thought about the sensation it would cause, the harder it became to hold your tongue. So you finally served it up with all the trimmings, making out of some man's personal tragedy and his relatives' pain a delicious feast of gossip.

Beneath all of the mechanism we have discussed lies one basic reason for gossip. We gossip because we fail to love. When we love people, we don't criticize them. "Love covers all offenses" (Prov 10:12). If we love them, their failures hurt. Paul says, "Love . . . does not rejoice at wrong" (1 Cor 13:5-6). We don't advertise the sins of people we love any more than we advertise our own. In fact, if we love somebody, we'll be very slow even to believe wrong about him or her. We'll be so anxious to believe the best that we'll be reluctant to face the damning facts. We'll automatically play lawyer for the defense.

No Wood for the Fire

If tearing others down is a temptation, how can we overcome it? First, by not listening to gossip or criticism. When we listen, we increase the gossip's sense of importance. We give him or her an audience.

This is hard advice. We may really *want* to listen. And it is embarrassing to cut someone's gossip off in midstream. But we can be tactful in the way we do it. We might say, "Look, Bob, the Lord's shown me that I have a weakness for looking out for other people's failures. He's been dealing with me about it. If you don't mind, we'd better change the subject." Make the break clean. We will have made Bob search his own conscience, and what's more, it will dawn on him someday that if we won't listen to his gossip about someone else, neither will we listen to someone else's gossip about him. He'll respect us for it.

My mother had an infallible method for coping with

gossips and critics. I'll never forget the day when the lady next door was dripping vitriol about the neighbor on the far side. My mother took hold of her neighbor's arm. "Come on," she said, "let's go and talk to her about it." It was the last time our next-door neighbor ever criticized another neighbor in my mother's presence.

She did the same with all the neighbors. Did she miss out on all the gossip? Well, maybe she did. I never asked her. But what she lost in back-fence gossip she gained in out-poured confidences. The women knew they could come to her with a personal problem or a heartache. They could trust her tongue. She probably had a more accurate, if less lurid, knowledge of a lot that went on in the neighborhood.

I also recommend dealing with the feeling of criticism while it's still unspoken. Is the criticism real or imaginary? Does it deal with some grave sin in somebody, or is it just something that grates us the wrong way? Whichever it is, we should take it to the Lord before we talk to anyone else. Read Proverbs 26:20 as you pray: "For lack of wood the fire goes out; and where there is no whisperer, quarreling ceases."

If our criticism concerns Jim Black, let's go first to Jim Black. Remember Paul's recommendation in Galatians about how we should approach Jim. "You who are spiritual should restore him in a spirit of gentleness. Look to yourself, lest you too be tempted" (Gal 6:1).

It may be that distasteful information will have to be imparted to other Christians as well. Their well-being and the purity of the church may be involved. But let us ask these questions: Am I absolutely sure of the facts? Is there any beam in my own eye? Do I love this person—not in word only but in deed and in truth? What is the best way of dealing with the problem? (The best way will never be to spill the beans to all your best friends first.) Is there scriptural direction on how to deal with it?

Retrieving Feathers

Finally, if there is no need to talk, be silent. Keep quiet when the person's name comes up. Ask God to set a watch on your lips (Ps 141:3).

Once a young man spread around a piece of criticism (which later proved only half-true) about his elderly pastor which split the church and created a scandal. He later apologized and asked the old man what he could do to atone for his wrong. The pastor grabbed a feather pillow under his arm and took the fellow to the top of the church tower. Wind tugged at their hair, flapping their coattails against their legs as they looked giddily at the village and fields below them. The pastor handed the young man the pillow.

"Rip it open," he said.

The boy was perplexed. But he did what he was told. Instantly the wind seized the feathers, tossing them in flurries into the air. A cloud of feathers whirled about their heads, then spread far and wide as thousands of feathers began falling beyond the village, settling on sidewalks, in hedges, in streams, in trees, among deep grass.

"Now," said the pastor, "go and collect all the feathers and put them back in the pillow."

"*All* of them?"

"*All* of them."

"But that's impossible!"

Placing his hand on the young boy's shoulder, the pastor said kindly, "I know. I just wanted you to realize how impossible it is to retrieve a criticism once spoken."

When you are tempted to criticize another person, remember this story. "He who goes about as a talebearer reveals secrets, but he who is trustworthy in spirit keeps a thing hidden" (Prov 11:13).

26
Fiction
Addiction

_____Fiction used to be an escape for me. I took to it like an alcoholic to whiskey. When problems or unwelcome tasks made life unpleasant, I could slide through an invisible doorway into a private dream world where both my friends' voices and my conscience became muted and distant. Reading was a kind of debauchery. I read compulsively, voraciously. Each morning I groped under my pillow for the book I'd been reading the night before.

I even had literary hangovers. Emerging from my reading depressed, irritable and absent-minded, reality would seem flatter, problems greater and unwelcome tasks more unbearable. Prayer would become a chore; Bible reading, lifeless. Unconsciously I would look for escape in the Bible, but since the Bible was not designed as a means of escape, it let me down.

I was aware of my problem and made serious attempts to solve it. Confining my reading to the works of acknowledged masters, I parried the thrusts of my conscience by pointing out that I was absorbing culture. But even literary masterpieces can be used as a means of escape. Eventually my "controlled" reading became less controlled. After a while anything would serve: classics, "Christian" fiction, detective stories, love stories. The most discerning connoisseurs of wines will drink methylated spirits if they become desperate alcoholics. They drink because they have to, not because they enjoy it. My reading had become like that.

Eventually God changed me, and my cultural loss was insignificant beside my spiritual gain. My solution was the same as the alcoholic's: total abstinence. I took down from my bookshelves every work of fiction (allowing myself only nonfiction works and allegories—Bunyan, Lewis and a few others), lovingly packed the precious volumes into an enormous crate, and gave the whole lot to a friend who was studying English literature. (I'm not sure which was greater, his bewilderment or his gratitude.)

It was like throwing open the windows and doors of my mind to reality's warm sun and fresh air. I stopped dreaming and began to live. It was a major step forward in my spiritual life.

I'm not suggesting, however, that in order to become more spiritual everyone must do the same. My point is simply that fiction (whether in books or in movies) is an uncontrollable escape mechanism for some Christians. It may have started innocently by enjoying Tolkien but turned into a consuming addiction to fantasy in general. In such cases its harmful effects are much greater than its benefits. If this is true of you, then I *do* recommend total abstinence. For you, reading fiction or going to a movie may represent temptation. The biblical recommendation is that we flee temptation, not that we try to control it.

Fresh Problems

That was years ago. I no longer have such a great need for escape as I had then. I've discovered that it never pays to run away from life, but that life, especially when lived in fellowship with Jesus Christ, holds deep joy and solid satisfaction. I'm now too busy doing things I enjoy to want to escape.

I can't remember how I began reading fiction again, except that abstinence gradually ceased to be a matter of importance. When I read, I found that fiction had less fascination for me, that I was more critical of what I read. I read for relaxation, not for escape, though to be honest there are still times (perhaps I've been overworking or am under strain) when I am aware that the line between relaxation and escape is hard to distinguish. Of course, I still have to be careful with fiction. But now my problem is when to read and what to read.

I cannot adopt "Christian fiction and no other kind" as a rule of thumb. I have found that some "Christian" fiction is Christian only in the sense that it sentimentalizes the gospel. Much of it is sanctimonious trash in which the girl both becomes a Christian and gets the fellow (perhaps not the original fellow, but always the nicest one).

The contrast between bad fiction or film making by Christians and good fiction or film making by non-Christians set me thinking about what makes it good or bad. Literature professors could doubtless give clearer criteria, but I have been thinking the matter out for myself as a Christian. I'm not qualified to suggest criteria by which "good" literature or "good" movies can be measured, but as a Christian I'm beginning to discern what is good for me. Among the things I appreciate are reality, sincerity and the ability to portray a truly human problem with both charity and clarity.

Reality

By reality I mean faithfulness in portraying life as it is rather than rearranging life to make it what the writer would like it to be (which is what many "Christian" writers do). A literary critic commented that as you finished reading *War and Peace,* Tolstoy's masterpiece, you said, "That's life!" This quality demands not only unique powers of observation and insight, but a kind of disciplined honesty in writing. I appreciate realism in literature and film because it helps me look at life and myself with clearer eyes than I am sometimes able to do on my own.

But realism itself raises problems. Realistic writing doesn't evade sin, and I've had to face the question of how profitable it is to read about sin. It's a touchy subject, and once again it would be easy for me to make a flat rule to avoid any books or movies that refer, say, to sexual sin. But in practice such a rule is hard to apply. There is an infinite gradation from oblique allusion to frankly erotic description. The same is true of references to brutality and hatred. Moreover, the Bible doesn't ignore sinful acts. Purity in thought, evidently, is something more profound than merely closing one's eyes to sin.

Sexual sin and temptation are an integral part of life as we experience it. They are woven into the tangled problems of life in the same way as pride and ambition. Ignoring sexual problems in art (just as ignoring them in life) is itself to fantasize of a world that doesn't exist.

Of course, there are ways of dealing with certain matters which are realistic yet chaste. A great deal depends on the writers' attitudes. As I read I look at life through their eyes. Ideally, in their own minds, they should neither condone the sin nor condemn the sinner.

Nevertheless I find I must avoid all reading that in any way sexually stimulates me or diminishes my horror of sin. The same is true for movie going. However justified the writer was in writing as he did, I know I'm not justified in reading it if I begin to elicit even the mildest sexual pleasure from it. And this happens. My problem at this point (especially if I am away from home) is that a kind of sexual chain reaction can start up, which leads from erotic images to sexual tension. I believe I am fairly normal in this.

Sincerity

Sincerity has a purifying effect on what a writer writes. By sincerity I mean the honesty with which the writer *addresses* me rather than merely plays on my emotions. Some writers (just like some preachers) have made such a habit of being insincere that they are unaware of the tricks they employ. Their whole outlook is governed by a desire to produce an effect on the reader. Their aim is not so much to share an insight (some have none to share) as to shock, dazzle or harrow the reader. Exaggeration, crude sensationalism and appeals to self-pity may be used in this way. So may pornography.

Writers of romance novels might adopt the practice of harrowing me with the cruel sufferings of the genteel heroine. In pitying the heroine I am really pitying myself, as I tearfully imagine wicked people and frightful coincidences reducing me to extremities of misunderstanding and abuse. Whatever the device, authors are playing on my weaknesses. They are tickling me in my emotional ribs, and like a dog I stretch my limbs in an ecstasy of appreciation. They know what I want, and they shamelessly make themselves my accomplice. Their insincerity and my weakness are our mutual undoing.

Such devices are not needed to secure my interest. Life itself is fascinating. Real people are absorbing if seen through perceiving eyes. Good writers use vision where bad ones employ tricks. When I put down a good book I am humbled. I find myself saying, "That is me all over but I've never realized it before." One book offers me an escape from myself while another shows me myself or my neighbors in a way that helps me understand them better. All this is just as true of films. Having seen *Gandhi*, I shall never feel the same about India.

Human Problems

I realize that stories, with the exception of allegories, are not tracts. But at the same time I appreciate those that deal kindly and realistically with human problems. It is here that Christian fiction on the whole has failed. Some people may object to my remark about the heroines in the "Christian" novel getting the "best" man. After all, doesn't God give us the best if we leave the choice to him?

True enough. But what constitutes "the best"? The most handsome husband? The most talented? And how do these couples in "Christian" fiction face life? What kinds of doubts and problems beset them once they're married? How understanding are their Christian friends? How do they manage their children? In real life couples sin, face severe difficulties and even fail. Pastors find themselves counseling many such couples, but rarely is this represented in "Christian" fiction.

Yet my purpose isn't to criticize Christian literature, but to explain why I personally often prefer certain non-Christian writers who seem both more sincere and more truthful.

Detective Stories

Some of my friends have asked whether I ever read whodunits. Yes, occasionally, especially when I'm tired or want a break. Detective stories seldom provide new insights into human problems. They are written for entertainment; and if I read them, I read them as such. I think of them in the same category as crossword puzzles, but to me they are much more interesting.

Yet even in this I have to be discerning. Many modern mysteries glory in the seamy facets of life, in dirt, dames, dope, dipsomania. I like realism—when realism serves a useful purpose. But I read detective stories for entertainment; and I dare not find entertainment in dirt. My favorite mystery writers (I don't profess to be an expert) are G. K. Chesterton, Dorothy Sayers and Agatha Christie.

Art and Morality

Reading fiction and going to movies are two of many activities about which the Bible gives no specific commands. I have tried to spotlight problems and clarify one or two principles. All of us should open our Bibles to think and pray about our own attitudes. The Bible, although it does not give specific commands, does deal with attitudes and principles that can be applied to fiction as well as to any other part of modern life. Let me mention a few by asking some questions.

Is it my master? If so, I should remember that no one can serve two masters, for he will love one and hate the other (Mt 6:24).

Does it help me escape from life, or does it point me to life? My loins should be girded about with truth (Eph 6:14). Among other things, truth implies a certain attitude to life, an attitude in which I continually face myself as I am, and my neighbors and God as they are. I don't escape to a world of illusion. On the other hand, I welcome anything that helps me see more clearly.

Is it wholesome? As a general rule it is desirable for me to think about pure things, lovely things, things of good report (Phil 4:8). I cannot altogether avoid thinking of sin, nor is this the purpose behind Paul's recommendation. But is my thinking about sin wholesome and constructive? Will it sharpen my sensitivity to sin, or help me to deal more understandingly with others who get tangled in it? Some works of fiction may be of real service here. Others are definitely an anesthesia to our conscience.

Am I (with books and movies as well as everything else)

being a good steward of my time? Do I read fiction when I should be praying? (Honesty but not morbid introspection or superspiritual pietism is what I need at this point.)

If the ultimate aim of my life is to know Christ, to what extent does it contribute to or impede my progress in this direction?

Some friends of mine who study art place great stress on "artistic integrity." They seem to view an artist's creative activity as amoral. "Let him be true to his art and he will produce something of intrinsic value. Don't measure its value with an ethical yardstick. That would be like condemning a carpet because it can't be used for a kleenex."

The argument is out of focus with Christian truth. Artistic creations represent human activity. Human activity takes place within a moral framework, for "in him [a Moral Being] we [whether Christian or non-Christian] live and move and have our being" (Acts 17:28). Our lives and activities can only be evaluated properly when viewed in relation to God. We can no more take such activity out of its moral context than we can take ourselves outside God's sovereignty.

More to the point (for I'm not primarily concerned with artistic values per se), the book or movie or play does produce an effect on me. Whatever its artistic quality, it influences me (for good or ill) when I interact with it.

In a coming day when my life is reviewed and its actions tried by fire, I shall give account of how I used my mind and body, and why.

I am thinking out my answers now.

27
Tickle-and-Tease: The Lure of Pornography

_____How about pornography? Some Christians feel strongly that to indulge in it is sin. Others feel equally strongly that, even while pornographic reading may not itself be sin, its indulgence opens the way to sin.

Pornography can be defined as visual material, chiefly literature and film, designed to produce erotic stimulation. Pornography offers sensual delights to the man or woman who fails to find enough delight in flesh-and-blood relationships. But at what cost? How delightful *is* the product? What can it do for me? Is it worth the psychological price? If not, how are we to explain the grip it has on some people?

Pornography is a tickle-and-tease. If you like being tickled and teased, you will like pornography. But tickle-and-tease gets you nowhere except hankering after more tickle-and-tease. It does not satisfy in the way a meal satisfies an appetite, and certainly not in the way sexual intercourse can be fulfilling in a love relationship. It is the itch you can never scratch enough.

Scratching an itch is ecstasy that never satisfies, hence its maddeningly ongoing nature. You never have enough to be satisfied. Pornography is the ultimate dangling carrot.

Let me go further. Experiments show that the relationship between sensory stimulation and pleasure is not static. The more sensual stimulation we are exposed to, the greater our tolerance of it becomes. And the greater our tolerance of stimulation, *the more of it we require to achieve pleasure*.

If I get a kick out of hot mustard and use it regularly, I'll need to take more to get the same kick out of it, just as a heroin addict needs a bigger fix to get the same "rush." That's why I call pornography the ultimate dangling carrot. In the end one has to work harder to get less.

The Fantasy Factor

Pornography fosters conscious or even unconscious hopes for the ultimate sexual experience in the form of a fantasy love nest, or even of multiple and bizarre forms of sexual interactions. If you are rich you may acquire the accouterments, the setting, the implements and the beautiful, sensual partner(s). The experience will probably lead to increasing boredom, but most of us are not rich enough to discover this.

Most pornography addicts have to close their eyes to their real partners during sexual relations while they struggle to recapture the vision of a centerfold. (In doing so, they are not really having sexual relations. Communion is absent. Two bodies are moving toward climax, each absorbed in isolated fantasies.) People who lack sexual partners may creep away with a photograph to masturbate in the toilet. What looks glamorous on glossy paper usually proves sordid in practice.

You can see at once that if we think about the purpose of sex (the ending of aloneness and the developing of a deep and intimate relationship—not to mention creating children, home and family), pornography is a cheat and a hindrance. Our moral evaluation of it begins at this point. Pornography destroys what God designed—a relationship between husband and wife that reflects God's own relationship with all of us.

Pornography has other deleterious effects. It can, over the long haul, make married people increasingly dissatisfied with their conjugal relations. Sexual responses are learned. That is to say, married people can become progressively more responsive to the erotic stimulus provided by each other. Changes take place in their central nervous systems so that their responses become more complementary. They adapt to each other. Their mutual sensual pleasures grow. They are like dancers whose practice together makes them better partners, not only in bed but in daily living.

The Rotten Core

Pornography is innately evil, evil not because of any deleterious effects it might produce but because it is hostile to God's purposes for human sexuality. It destroys human dignity. It is *a dangling carrot with a rotten core*. To say that its evil lies in its tendency to "open the way to sexual sin" is to weaken the arguments against it. It may be true to say that some people who indulge in pornography at one stage in their lives become promiscuous later. I am less convinced that the relationship is a cause-and-effect one.

I know, for instance, of one man who gets a kick out of reading skin books and who does so immediately before he indulges in his own brand of sexual immorality. But as I discuss the matter with him, I find his mind is really made up before he ever goes to the magazine stand. The dialog with himself runs something like this:

Man: "I think I'll thumb through some girlie books."

Conscience: "You know what happens when you do that, don't you?"

Man: "Yeah, I know. But let's not think about that. Let's

just look at the girlie books for now."

He does not allow his real goals to enter his awareness at the pornography stage. But once he's had his appetizer, he proceeds to the main course—which was what he intended to do all along.

It is also true that pornography reflects an attitude to sexuality, to members of the opposite sex, and that it tends to be associated with a certain lifestyle. You can't read it without vicariously experiencing the lifestyle in imagination. Sooner or later (and usually sooner) it drives the reader to be either two-faced or secretive. You can be two-faced in the sense that you act one way with fellow porn users and another with people who wouldn't "understand." Or else you can be a "closet porney"—one who lives a dangerous double life, is grateful for plain brown wrappers, and keeps the stuff hidden. I don't know anyone who is proud of being a closet porney.

In and of Itself

It may be true, and certainly I am in no position to prove the contrary, that some people would never have engaged in sexual sin had they not first indulged their fantasy with pornography. Evidence is growing in favor of the once disputed idea that freely available pornography correlates with increased sex crimes (see John Court, *Pornography: A Christian Critique*). But whatever the truth of the matter, I am not attracted to arguments based on expediency. Pornography is bad because of what it is, not just because of what it might lead to.

I must hasten to stand, however, with those who are dismayed by the power that tickle-and-tease seems to have over them. I find that my own eyes like to stray where my conscience tells them not to and that my juices are on the side of my eyes rather than on the side of my conscience. Am I a freak? Am I a dirty old man?

Well, I suppose I could be both if I let myself be. But at the point where I am (pleasurably) jolted by the magazine racks as I buy my newspaper, I am still a free being. God has set me free. I therefore, like Job, have made a covenant with my eyes not to look where they should not look and with my mind not to play games with what I inadvertently (or even deliberately) saw.

My covenant will not always be easy to keep, bearing in mind the impudent liveliness of my eyes and my juices. It will be wise for me to think carefully what my lifelong covenant with my eyes will mean. Let me not set out to build a tower without counting the cost. But count the cost I must. And, if I am wise, I will also seal the covenant.

28
The Problem of Christian Pain

Many think that the true Christian life should be trouble-free. When Paul in Galatians 5 speaks of the fruit of the Spirit's being joy, we too quickly jump to the conclusion that our lives are to be free of pain and full of happiness. When he speaks of peace, we assume an absence of storms.

Our natural reaction to personal tragedy is that something has gone profoundly wrong. We may have doubts about our whole relationship with God or feel that the Bible has been disproved or think that we are being punished. However, in Galatians 5 Paul is talking about character rather than experience. Jesus made a special point of warning the disciples repeatedly that their lives were to be ones of tribulation and suffering.

The Christian life is meant to be triumphant rather than trouble-free. The New Testament writers are united in pointing out that painful experiences are to be expected by all Christians. Paul even asserts, "We rejoice in our sufferings, knowing that suffering produces endurance, and endurance produces character" (Rom 5:3-4). James tells us, "Count it all joy, my brethren, when you meet various trials, for you know that the testing of your faith produces stead-fastness" (Jas 1:2-3). Peter writes, "You may have to suffer various trials, so that the genuineness of your faith . . . may redound to praise and glory and honor" (1 Pet 1:6-7).

All were speaking from personal experience. In compar-ing his lot with those of phony Christians, Paul says he has had "far greater labors, far more imprisonments, with countless beatings, and often near death. Five times I have received at the hands of the Jews the forty lashes less one. Three times I have been beaten with rods; once I was stoned. Three times I have been shipwrecked; a night and a day I have been adrift at sea; . . . in toil and hardship, through many a sleepless night, in hunger and thirst, often without food, in cold and exposure. And apart from other things, there is the daily pressure upon me of my anxiety for all the churches" (2 Cor 11:23-25, 27-28).

We respond, "Yes, but these things happened to Paul because he was a special case. He was a missionary in full-time Christian service. Right?" Wrong! These things hap-pened to Paul because he was obedient to Jesus. Jesus, Paul, the writer to the Hebrews, James and Peter all clearly teach that painful experiences for Christians is normal. The ques-tions we must face are: Why should this be so? And, what should our attitude be when "tragedy," major or minor, strikes?

The Problem
The immediate sources of Paul's sufferings (like those of Jesus) were evil. Evil people with evil motives inspired by the Evil One succeed in making the lives of faithful Chris-tians difficult. They always have. They always will.

Natural catastrophes also occur—storms at sea, danger in travel. Sickness or poverty can also come our way, or we become victims (just as do non-Christians) of the general injustices of the system. Finally our own sin and stupidity may cause our pain.

But in the final analysis all suffering arises out of evil. Why should we be expected to rejoice when evil causes us pain? Is God not greater than evil? If so, why does he not prevent it? And if he fails to prevent it, is he not in a way collaborating with it? How can it be right to thank him when evil triumphs?

The problem is the toughest of all theological problems to understand. Briefly stated, it can be expressed in the following propositions:

1. While God accepts ultimate responsibility for evil, he is not its source.

2. God could have prevented the occurrence of all evil, but to have done so *and* given humans and angels freedom would have been *intrinsically* impossible. He had to opt either for angelic and human robots, or for beings who could choose—and who therefore could choose evil. He couldn't have it both ways. Even God could not "have his cake and eat it."

3. God retains, however, ultimate control of evil. Such is his sovereignty that he brings good out of it. Out of the injustice and Satanic hatred of Calvary he bought our redemption and our deliverance from death. Human and angelic evil will ultimately be self-destructive; they will be judged and seen to have served the ends of greater good.

4. Any evil that touches us does so with God's consent, and it is for our good. It does not usually represent punishment but potential character gain, the privilege of sharing in Christ's sufferings, or both of these.

5. Pain has as much potential for blessing in our lives as it has for harm.

To these last two propositions I now turn my attention.

Rejoice Is a Verb

"We rejoice in our sufferings, knowing that suffering produces endurance, and endurance produces character, and character produces hope." We rejoice. This is not to say that we experience spontaneous feelings of pleasure. We are not called to be masochists. "For the moment all discipline seems painful rather than pleasant" (Heb 12:11). *Rejoice* is a verb. It means to adopt a specific attitude. *Happiness* and *pleasure* are nouns. We can't *happy*. But we can rejoice. How?

We can deliberately recognize the fact that God knows what is happening to us, that he is not trying to be mean (no good parent enjoys having to give small children their swats) and that he has a plan behind the experience, a plan for our well-being. We can and should deliberately thank him, not for the suffering itself, but for his faithful control of it and his blessed purpose in allowing it. Our confidence in him at this point will actually halve the pain, and may even make it negligible.

And what is the purpose behind the suffering? "Knowing that suffering produces endurance . . ." Spontaneous faith, faith on the spur of the moment, is useful. What is more necessary for a true disciple of Jesus, however, is steadfast, unwavering faith, faith that holds on when times are tough. Such faith can only develop one way, and that is through suffering. Suffering produces endurance. Nothing is more necessary to us than *enduring* faith.

"And endurance produces character . . ." Earlier I said Paul's remarks in Galatians 5 have to do with character rather than with experience. Individual character is forged on an anvil of pain. It is not mass produced. In ancient times the purest gold was produced by heat, heat carefully and repeatedly applied.

The teaching of James and of Peter is identical with Paul's. After exhorting us to rejoice in trials because they can produce steadfastness, James writes, "And let steadfastness have its full effect, that you may be perfect and complete, lacking in nothing" (Jas 1:4). He is talking about character building, hinting that there is no short cut to it. Steadfast faith is itself a road to a goal—the goal of a mature, stable, rounded character. Most of us lack such a character. To build it within us is God's goal. His project will continue throughout our lives. And his instruments will involve us in pain.

The Two-edged Sword

There are two sides to pain. It has as much potential for character destruction as for character building. The pain that makes robust saints can equally well create embittered, defeated cynics. Everything depends on the sufferer's response.

Before plastic surgery became technically sophisticated, a famous film star damaged her lovely face in a car accident. The surgeon explained that the damage could be repaired and her beauty restored but that the operation would have to be carried out (for certain technical reasons) without any anesthetic. She had to choose between pain and her career on the one hand or no pain and no career on the other. She chose pain.

During the operation the actress's cooperation was vital. It meant remaining perfectly still during moments of extreme suffering. When a scalpel was carefully shaping a rounded curve of skin, a sudden move of her head would have increased the damage. In actual fact the reconstruction of a beautiful face was accomplished by collaboration between the surgeon and the actress.

It is much the same in the Christian life. The pain we suffer does not produce automatic results. As the writer to the Hebrews puts it, "Later it yields the peaceful fruit of righteousness *to those who have been trained by it*" (Heb 12:11). Those who have not been trained by pain are usually damaged by it. To be trained by it means to have adopted a believing, rejoicing, thankful attitude whenever frustration, pain or even what from a human perspective would be viewed as tragedy and catastrophe occur.

The range of its forms and of its severity is infinite. My wife spilled blueberries all over a pale green carpet while I was in the middle of the previous sentence. Cars that won't start or that stall in the middle of an intersection and a thousand petty annoyances as well as indescribable horrors are included. All come by God's sovereign purpose. The results depend on the ways we habitually respond.

Loving Our Enemies

The matter of our response to pain goes even further. I mentioned that hurt may come to us in the form of persecution. Our persecutors may be enemies of the gospel, or they may be our fellow Christians. No pain is so bewildering as injustice or cruelty from a brother or sister in Christ. Yet if we are to be thankful to God, we cannot at the same time give way to resentment and bitterness toward those who have made themselves our enemies. A test of whether we have truly understood the principle, of whether we are genuinely obedient to it, will be found in our attitude to the human "enemies" who cause our pain.

If we keep this in mind, loving our enemies may not be as difficult as it would at first appear. If we can see an enemy as someone who is an unwitting instrument of our blessing, it will be much easier to be forgiving and loving toward that person.

Joseph's brothers hated him, plotted to murder him, then sold him into slavery in Egypt to face alienation from all that he loved. Later, as master of Egypt, Joseph held the power of revenge between his fingers. Yet when his brothers, knowing his power and fearing him, lied to him, Joseph wept and said, "Fear not, for am I in the place of God? *As for you, you meant evil against me; but God meant it for good.* . . . So do not fear; I will provide for you and your little ones" (Gen 50:19-21).

His brothers intended evil. And Joseph did suffer. But God intended (and delivered) only good, not just to Joseph but to millions of people. We can love our enemies if we discover that they can never truly harm us. They can only, while they may not appear to do so, be agents of God's blessing to us and to others.

There is, of course, the little matter of pain we suffer because of our own stupidity or our own sin. How do we respond to that? In essentially the same way. Naturally, we must acknowledge our sin and folly to God. Naturally, we will thank him for his pardon. But our sin may give rise to certain painful and unwelcome consequences. If we are silly enough to make lying boasts, we may later face painful humiliation. The word *discipline* may be substituted for the word *suffering* here; but, whichever word is used, the pain comes from a loving hand—with a loving purpose. And for these things we must thank God. We must even rejoice.

Is it easy to respond to pain with joy? No, but it can be learned. Is it worthwhile? Infinitely so. Not only may we be collaborating with God in his kindness toward us, but (in persecution) we will have the privilege of sharing in the very sufferings of Christ.

Let us then "consider him who endured from sinners such hostility against himself, so that [we] may not grow weary or fainthearted" (Heb 12:3). Let us look "to Jesus the pioneer and perfecter of our faith, who for the joy that was set before him endured the cross, despising the shame, and is seated at the right hand of the throne of God" (Heb 12:2). Amen.

Notes

Chapter 5: Christ: Born of a Virgin
[1] See Norman Anderson, *The Mystery of the Incarnation* (Downers Grove, Ill.: InterVarsity Press, 1978), pp. 26, 30, 95-100.

Chapter 6: Christ: Died on a Cross
[1] Gustav Aulen, *Christus Victor* (New York: Macmillan, 1969).
[2] B. F. Westcott, "The Epistles of St. John" (1883), pp. 34-37, quoted in A. M. Stibbs, *The Meaning of the Word "Blood" in Scripture* (London: Tyndale Press, 1962).
[3] Stibbs, *The Meaning*, p. 15.
[4] Philip Bliss, "Man of Sorrows."

Chapter 17: God's Perfect Peace
[1] Horatius Bonar, *God's Way of Holiness* (Chicago: Moody Press, n.d.), p. 3.

Chapter 19: The Gift of Guidance
[1] C. S. Lewis, *The Magician's Nephew* (New York: Macmillan, 1955), pp. 141-42.

Read on for further titles in the

JOHN WHITE LIBRARY

The Cost of Commitment

JOHN WHITE

'For years I felt guilty because I never seemed to be committed deeply enough to Christ... I had the feeling that I should be suffering more, doing without more. Yet when I did suffer, my suffering bore little relationship to my commitment. Sometimes it seemed to arise from my lack of commitment and at other times bore no relation at all to it...

'When Jesus tells you to take up your cross daily, he is not telling you to find some way to suffering daily. He is simply giving forewarning of what happens to the person who follows him.'

A warm and personal book to help Christians count the cost of commitment.

"...message is presented in a lucid, readable, at times very moving style.."   Evangelical Times

".. useful book to place into the hands of those who have recently made the great decision."
                                        Christian Herald

91 pages   Pocketbook

Inter-Varsity Press

Eros Defiled

JOHN WHITE

To be human is to be sexual. That's the way God made us.

Yet many people – Christians included – are tormented by their sexuality. The problem may be frustration, masturbation, premarital sex and perhaps pregnancy, an 'affair', homosexuality, or strange compulsions.

To these people and their counsellors, John White offers compassion, help and hope.

"… a refreshing direct book. It.. shows a great deal of sensitivity, and has no fear of straight speaking."   Christian Weekly Newspapers

"The book's arguments are carefully anchored in the Bible. Undoubtedly *Eros Defiled* should be required reading for all in the pastoral ministry… Youth leaders… parents too. It can be recommended also to Christian adolescents in their late teens."   Evangelical Times

168 pages   Pocketbook

Inter-Varsity Press

The Fight

JOHN WHITE

John White has written this book because he wants you to understand clearly what the Christian life is all about. He wants you to learn in the depths of your being that the eternal God loves you and plans only your highest good – more trust in him, more likeness to him.

But his love will bring pain as intense as your joy. For the Christian life is a fight....

"Reading *The Fight* is to inhale great draughts of fresh air into one's Christian life... This is the kind of book every 20th Century Christian should have on his book shelf."

Christian Weekly Newspapers

230 pages   Pocketbook

Inter-Varsity Press

The Masks of Melancholy

JOHN WHITE

Depression wears many masks. One sufferer just feels 'down'; another slashes his veins in lonely despair. Some whirl along in manic euphoria; others move with limbs of lead.

What is this monster that enslaves so many victims?
Is it spiritual? Physical? Demonic?
Why do Christians suffer too?
Why do people kill themselves?
How effective are today's therapies – counselling, drugs, ECT – and how do they work?

John White tackles these questions with the expertise of an experienced psychiatrist and the wisdom of a Christian steeped in God's Word. He offers guidance and encouragement to all who care for the depressed, whether as doctors, counsellors, pastors, friends or relatives.

"...this is a much needed book."   Today

"Distressed people need hope. This book is a means of encouraging that hope."   Renewal

252 pages   Pocketbook

Inter-Varsity Press

Parents in Pain

JOHN WHITE

Are you a parent?
How will you react if your child gets involved in
drugs, crime, sleeping around, alcoholism?
Will you blame yourself? your child?
society?

Whether you are a parent, potential parent, or
friend, this book will help you. It describes what
you can do and what you can't. Recognising the
limits of your responsibility will save you from
needless anguish and self-blame. This is a book
to help you meet difficulties with courage and
confidence.

"..offers the kind of help no Christian parent can
afford to miss."   Family (formerly Life of Faith)

"This is an important book…"   Renewal

242 pages   Pocketbook

Inter-Varsity Press

People in Prayer

JOHN WHITE

Ten portraits of people in prayer to God.

People pleading, praising, confessing, interceding. People being changed as they draw closer to God.

God – wanting communication with human beings. With you.

"Go after this book – get it and read it! It will challenge and disturb but you will not regret it."
Grace Magazine

"…the contents proved so helpful. At all times practical, open, and in touch with our own times." Reaper (New Zealand)

"This is a wholesome book, penetrating in its insight and profound in its encouragements."
Life and Work

"It is impossible to read this book without being driven to the Master's feet, with one simple petition, "Lord, teach us to pray"."
Christian Herald

160 pages   Pocketbook

Inter-Varsity Press